SPIRAL GUIDES

Travel With Someone You Trust®

W9-BLC-391

DOMINICAN REPUBLIC

Contents

Written by Ron Emmons

Copy edited by Colin Hinshelwood
Verified by Colin Hinshelwood
Indexed by Ron Emmons
Pages designed by Douglas E. Morton,
CPA Media, Chiang Mai, Thailand

Edited, designed and produced by AA Publishing
© Automobile Association Developments Limited 2005
Maps © CPA Media 2005

Published in the United States by AAA Publishing,
1000 AAA Drive, Heathrow, Florida 32746
Published in the United Kingdom by AA Publishing

ISBN 1-59508-036-8

Cover design and binding style by permission of AA Publishing

Color separation by Keenes, Andover
Printed and bound in China by Leo Paper Products

10 9 8 7 6 5 4 3 2 1

A01753

the magazine

The Dominican Melting Pot

I t only takes a quick glance around at the people of the Dominican Republic (commonly referred to in English as the DR) to realise that this is a country of great racial diversity. Indeed, the country's history is a bewildering catalogue of conquest and rebellion, of which the following facts are but a few of the highlights.

Taíno petroglyphs found at the caves of Las Caritas

The Friendly People

The first known inhabitants of the country, the **Taínos**, arrived around AD 800 in long, dugout canoes from their ancestral homeland in the Orinoco Delta, now part of Venezuela.

They called their new land *Ayiti*, meaning "Land of the Mountains", which is the origin of the name Haiti. The Taínos, whose name means "the friendly people", had a sophisticated social structure. They lived in communities of around 1,000–2,000 people on the coast or beside rivers, under the leadership of a *cacique* (chief), who could be either male or female. Their legacy lingers today only in the form of pictographs (wall pictures) and petroglyphs (wall carvings) in caves around the country, plus a few ceremonial artefacts now on display in museums.

The Spanish Conquest

When Christopher Columbus sighted the north coast of the island he was to name Hispaniola in December 1492, he noted it was "filled with trees of a thousand kinds and tall,

Taínospeak

Though the "Friendly people" were wiped out, a few of their words live on:

Taíno	English
barbacoa	barbecue
tabaco	tobacco
hamaca	hammock
huracán	hurricane
canoa	canoe
maíz	maize or corn

seeming to touch the sky". He established a settlement at La Navidad, in modern day Haiti, but later switched to La Isabela, further to the east, near Puerto Plata in the DR. Neither of these settlements was successful, but finally in 1496, Christopher's brother, Bartholemew, led the few remaining settlers south to found La Nueva Isabela, which continues to thrive to this day as Santo Domingo, the nation's capital. The Taínos must have been shocked by their first encounter with these visitors from afar. The hospitable natives helped drag a Spanish wreck ashore only to find themselves forced at knife and gun point to perform the Spaniards' bidding. This included finding gold, and when the expected riches did not appear, the invaders' mood grew even uglier. Taínos were massacred at random, and within a few decades, they were all but eliminated, either due to the conditions of slavery or through European diseases such as smallpox. Once the Spanish had established a base in the Americas, they quickly set about colonising Jamaica, Cuba, Puerto Rico and Mexico.

Taíno chiefs welcome Christopher Columbus

Local chieftain, Enriquillo, led a revolt against the Spanish in 1519

Pirates of the Caribbean

Since the Spanish could not police the vast oceans, it was not long before pirate ships began to appear on the horizon, attacking galleons laden with booty from Peru and Mexico and making off with precious cargo (▶ 16). When Havana superseded Santo Domingo in the mid-16th century as the most convenient port for Spanish fleets to assemble before heading back to Spain, Hispaniola became a backwater of the growing Spanish Empire, and piracy became rife.

Independence at Last

The fortunes of Santo Domingo floundered, so much so that by the early 18th century its population was less than 10,000. In the second half of that century however, many immigrants arrived from the Canary Islands as well as slaves from Africa, and the sugar and tobacco industries began to turn a profit. In 1804, a surprising turn of events saw neighbouring Haiti gain independence from the French, becoming the world's first independent black republic. Then in 1822, Haiti occupied its neighbour for 22 years until 27 February 1844, when a long struggle for independence ended and the Dominican Republic was born.

Dominican heroes: Duarte, Sanchez and Mella at Puerte El Conde

A Country for Sale

Two of the principal *caudillos*, or warlords, in the Dominican Republic after 1844 were Pedro Santana and Buenaventura Baez, who seemed to take turns mounting coups and exiling each other. Eventually, Santana made a request for Spanish annexation, which was granted in 1861, though the Spanish withdrew hurriedly in 1865 due to a devastating outbreak of yellow fever. This plunged the Dominican Republic back into further chaos, and in an audacious moment in 1869, Baez sold the entire country for $150,000 to US President Ulysses S. Grant. If the US Congress had not rejected the deal, the Dominican Republic would be part of the USA today.

Pre-Columbian bone artefact

Two young Dominican women in national costume

The Era of the Goat

Known variously as *El Jefe* (the boss), *El Benefactor* (the benefactor), *El Generalísimo* (the great general) and *El Chivo* (the goat), Rafael Leonidas Trujillo rose from petty criminal to become one of the most ruthless dictators the world has ever known. From 1930–61 he held the country in a tyrannical grip, taking control of sugar estates, cattle ranches and any other businesses that took his fancy. He developed a reputation as a man who never slept, never sweated and never had a wrinkle in his uniform, and anyone suspected of opposing him was instantly disposed of. In one incident alone, he had around 20,000 Haitians who were working in the country slaughtered.

To enhance his deified image, he commanded that Santo Domingo be re-named Ciudad Trujillo (Trujillo City). He was supported by the US government because of his anti-Communist stance, but eventually his luck ran out, and he was assassinated in a high-speed car chase as he was returning from Santo Domingo to his home in San Cristóbal late one night. The chasing car that was used in the daring deed, riddled with retaliatory bullets, is now on display in the Museum of History and Geography at the Plaza de la Cultura in Santo Domingo.

The Great Dictator

The late 19th century saw the rise to power of a military strongman, Ulises Heureaux, but after his assassination in 1899 the country teetered on the brink of civil war. This situation caused concerns about regional security for the US, which eventually occupied the Dominican Republic in 1916 and administered the country through the US Navy until 1924. During this period, improvements were made to the education system and many highways were built. However, the US also trained a repressive National Police Force, out of whose ranks emerged a certain General Trujillo (above), who would use his training to

devastating effect during his 30 years in power.

A Taste of Democracy

Trujillo was succeeded by Joaquín Balaguer, who had appeared a perfect front man for him. Yet Balaguer had his own agenda, not so different from Trujillo's, and by means of rigged elections and ruthless removal of opposition voices, he remained in power on and off until 1996. In that year, the Dominican Republic's first ever free elections saw Leonel Fernández voted in as president, and he was followed by Hipólito Mejía in 2000. Just who will hold the reins of power after the 2004 election is anybody's guess.

The late dictator, Rafael Leonidas Trujillo

FIESTA TIME

Most Dominicans don't need a second invitation to let their hair down, and the long list of annual festivals in the country gives them an excuse almost every day of the year. This is largely due to the *fiestas patronales*, or patron saint days (➤ 13), when each town in the country takes the chance to celebrate for a whole week. The biggest annual festivals are **Carnival** (February) and the **Merengue Festival** in Santo Domingo (July), but there are plenty more, of which the following are the ones you are most likely to see.

January

• 1 – **Cocolo Festival**, San Pedro de Macorís. Wildly-dressed performers known as "mummers" act out dance dramas in the streets.

• 21 – **Virgen de Altagracia**, Higuey. The country's most important religious festival is to DR's patron saint and attracts pilgrims from all over the country, joining together in processions and offering prayers to the Virgin.

• 26 – **Duarte Day**, nationwide (celebrated on Monday closest to this date). Holiday in memory of Juan Pablo Duarte, architect of independence in 1844 and founding father of the Dominican Republic.

February

• **Every Sunday** – Carnival, nationwide. Everyone dons colourful jesters' outfits and runs around hitting each other over the head with pigs' bladders just for the fun of it. Celebrations in La Vega are particularly raucous.

• 27 – **Independence Day**, nationwide. Coinciding with the culmination of Carnival, Independence Day is marked

by a military parade and battle re-enactments in Santo Domingo.

March/April
• **Semana Santa** (Holy Week) is celebrated throughout the Dominican Republic. The Christian festivities coincide with a major Voodoo celebration. Parades and processions marking both take place around the country.

June
• First week – **Puerto Plata Cultural Festival**. Blues, jazz and folk musicians perform

and dancers entertain on the Malecón, while an arts and crafts fair takes place around Parque Central.

• Third week – **Cabarete Race Week**. Kitesurfers and windsurfers vie for prizes at Playa Encuentro, west of Cabarete, as wind and wave conditions approach ideal.

• 23 – **Saradunga Festival**, Baní. African-style dancing to the beat of tambora drums features in this African/Roman Catholic rite.

• 29 – **San Pedro Festival**, San Pedro de Macorís. More dance dramas from the gaily-clad mummers, similar to the festival on 1 January.

• **Latin Music Festival**, (no fixed dates) Three day event at Santo Domingo Olympic Stadium.

July
• **Merengue Festival**, Santo Domingo (also Boca Chica). Starting in the third week of July and continuing for two weeks, the Malecón is packed every night with revellers dancing to the country's favourite music (► 20)

August
• 16 – **Restoration Day**, nationwide. Marking a declaration of war against Spanish occupation in 1863, this

Left: A spectacular carnival mask

Below: Elaborate floats are paraded through the larger towns

mini-carnival features floats, eye-catching costumes and – of course – lots of dancing.

October

• First week – **Jazz Festival**, Sosúa and Cabarete. Not willing to stand in the shadow of Puerto Plata, these lively towns on the north coast play host to an annual jazz festival that attracts international artistes.

• Third week – **Puerto Plata Merengue Festival**. Not content with its Cultural Festival in June, Puerto Plata tries to outdo the capital with its *merengue* festival on the Malecón.

December

• 25 – **Christmas**, nation-wide. Since the great majority of Dominicans are Catholics, Christmas is one of the most important annual festivals, when families exchange presents and eat a special meal.

• 31 – **New Year's Eve**, nationwide. Year's end brings yet another opportunity for Dominicans to get out and party till dawn, at clubs, pubs and private parties.

Below: A colourful military parade marking Independence Day in Santo Domingo

Bottom: Women enjoying their *fiesta patronal* or local patron saint festival

Patron Saint Festivals

Every town in the country has its patron saint, and on an appointed date each year, locals celebrate their *fiesta patronal* (patron saint festival) with parades through the streets of town. The big day is often preceded by *novenas*, nine nights of all-night drumming and call-and-response singing. Yet mixed with the African music are Catholic icons. This syncretism, or intermingling of different beliefs, is typically Dominican, coming from the days when slaves associated their own gods with the Catholic saints of their masters, and worshipped both. If you are lucky enough to stumble onto one of these local festivals, you can witness this powerful blend of influences on Dominican culture.

The Best of The Dominican Republic

Best dining experience
Paparazzo in Santo Domingo (➤ 62) serves delicious food and will leave you drooling for more.

Best dancing experience
Either in one of the night-clubs along the **Malecón** in Santo Domingo (➤ 64), or on the street itself during festivals.

Best beaches
Playa Rincón (➤ 93) and **Playa Bonita** (➤ 95), both on the Samaná Peninsula. Imagine a bay of turquoise, limpid water, fringed by powder-soft sand and towering palms, and you're halfway there.

Most exciting ride
(by boat)…whale watching in **Bahía de Samaná** (➤ 90).
(white-water rafting)…down the **Río Yaque del Norte** in Jarabacoa (➤ 148).
(by horse)…to the **Salto El Limón** on the Samaná Peninsula (➤ 161).
(by 4WD vehicle)…from **Jarabacoa** to **Constanza**, or vice versa (➤ 168).

Most challenging walk
A minimum three-day trek to the top of **Pico Duarte**, at 3,087m (10,125 feet) the highest point in the Caribbean (➤ 170).

Top centre: Enjoying the delights of Playa Rincón

Above: *Merengue* dancers enjoying themselves on the Malecón, Santo Domingo

Left: Trekking to the top of Pico Duarte

You'll need to be fit for this, but the breath-taking views make for an unforgettable experience.

Most romantic view

Watching the sunset while riding on horseback along **Playa Bonita** on the Samaná Peninsula (➤ 95).

If you only go to one

...museum in Santo Domingo, make it the **Museo de las Casas Reales** (➤ 49). The re-creation of the royal court shows how Spanish emissaries lived here like kings in their own right.

...church or cathedral in the country, it should be the **Catedral de Santa María la Menor** in Santo Domingo (➤ 46). The most important historical edifice in the country is accentuated with ornate carvings and rich décor.

...coral reef, head for **Cayo Paraíso** near Punta Rucia in the north (➤ 76). The multicoloured fish and maze of coral create an underwater paradise for snorkellers.

...national park, make it the **Armando Bermúdez** in the Cordillera Central for

good hiking trails and bird-watching.

Best off-the-beaten track

Las Galeras, in the extreme northeast of the Samaná Peninsula (➤ 96) and Las Salinas, on the southwest coast near Baní (➤ 128). Both are ideal spots to escape the tourist hordes.

Top right: White-water rafting on the Río Yaque del Norte

Above: The magnificent Catedral de Santa María la Menor

Pirates and Buccaneers of Hispaniola

As the Spanish conquest of the Americas gained momentum during the 16th century, small groups of daring men began to attack the Spanish galleons heading back to Europe. These pirates, privateers and buccaneers recognised no authority but their own, and for decades terrorised the Spanish Main, as the shipping lane through the Caribbean was known.

Privateers were no different to pirates, except that they acted with the full backing of their governments. Buccaneers were named after the *boucan*, French for a curing or smoking frame used by bands of English and Frenchmen that hunted wild oxen on the north coast of Hispaniola. Using small, light vessels that were faster than the bulky galleons, the buccaneers would take their victims by surprise, murder or kidnap all the crew and make off with the booty. Their numbers grew steadily and by the mid-17th century, they had established a secure base on the island of Tortuga, just off the northwest coast of Hispaniola.

Pirates and buccaneers are often romanticised as being freedom fighters of the high seas, yet in reality they were 16th century terrorists who delighted in dreaming up ghastly tortures for their victims, such as roasting them on a spit while still alive. The Spanish attacked the buccaneer base on Tortuga several times, and finally the rogue community dispersed in the 1670s, though pirate attacks continued to be a threat in the region for over another century.

Sir Francis Drake, freebooter extraordinaire

Some of the pirates who were active around Hispaniola included Englishmen Willy Simmons, Jack Banister and John Rackham, as well as Roberto Cofresi from nearby Puerto Rico. Perhaps the best known of all though, was the privateer, **Sir Francis Drake**, who cruised into Santo Domingo harbour with a fleet of 20 ships in 1586 and met no opposition. The fleet dropped anchor and entered town for a month-long orgy of pillage and destruction, before sailing away with their hulls full of loot.

Though you are unlikely to see any Jolly Roger flags flying off the Dominican coast these days, piracy is still rife in the republic. These modern acts of piracy do not involve swashbuckling sword fights on the deck of a galleon, but more innocuous behaviour such as selling bootleg CDs on the streets of Santo Domingo.

◆ TO THE CAPTAIN AND QUARTERMASTER
   -TWO SHARES OF THE BOOTY
   TO THE MASTER GUNNER AND BOATSWAIN
   - ONE AND A HALF SHARES OF THE BOOTY
   TO ALL OTHERS
   - ONE SHARE OF THE BOOTY.

◆ ALL IMPORTANT DECISIONS ARE
   TO BE PUT TO A VOTE

◆ ANY MAN CAUGHT STEALING
   SHALL BE MAROONED

◆ ANY MAN WHO LOSES
   A LIMB IN BATTLE
   SHALL RECEIVE EXTRA BOOTY

Though buccaneers respected no governments, they were loyal to each other and made decisions democratically

A Taste for ...Indulgence

Caribbean rum and cigars are recognised as the best in the world, and within the Caribbean, the Dominican Republic is famed for the high quality of both products. Its three major rum brands battle for superiority of the local market, while Dominican cigars are exported all over the world.

Rum – a Profitable By-Product

If the discovery of rum had been the result of some long and complex process of alchemy, it would still be a great achievement, but the fact that this drink is little more than a by-product of the sugar crystallisation process makes it something of a miracle. The **molasses** that remain after this process are thinned down and left to stand for about 12 days, before being distilled and

Brugal, the country's leading rum producer

A Rum Drinker's Dictionary

Spanish	English
Ron	rum
Claro	clear
Dorado	golden
Añejo	aged
Cuba Libre	rum and coke
Coco Loco	rum with coconut juice
Un Servicio	a bottle of rum with coke and ice

blended. Finally, the rum is matured in **oak barrels** for at least a year.

The three Bs – Brugal, Bermúdez and Barceló companies – are in a constant struggle to lead the market, with Brugal (the sponsor of the DR's road signs no less!) currently out in front. However, to find your personal favourite, you'll have to check out the clear, golden and aged versions of each brand. Most people mix rum with coke, and a squeeze of lemon gives it extra zest.

Classy Cigars

The health hazards associated with smoking have made it less socially acceptable world-wide, yet cigars remain synonymous with affluence and luxury. The big cigar exporters in the DR encourage this image, and the fertile fields of the Cibao Valley continue to produce this big-leaved plant introduced by the Taínos in great quantities.

In fact, since the 1990s the Dominican Republic has been the **world's largest producer of cigars**, and a visit to a cigar factory, in Santiago or elsewhere, makes for an interesting hour or two.

If you think the cigar-making process is simple, you will be surprised when you visit a factory and see just how complex it really is. The leaves must first be left to ferment, then to age for **several years** before being used. A master blender then selects a mix of different leaves for each cigar, with some chosen for aroma, others for taste, and others just for their combustion rate. After initial mixing, the leaves are then pressed for some hours before a final rolling. The outer leaf is one with a particular elasticity that makes it easier to roll. The resulting cigar may be straight or curved, long or short, thin or fat, depending on what type of smoke is desired.

Both rum and cigars make very distinctive Dominican gifts to take back home. If you're not sure which brands to go for, perhaps you could ask for a pack of León Jiménez cigars and a bottle of Brugal añejo rum.

Cutting and rolling a tobacco leaf

Tobacco leaves hung to age

One of the most exciting features of the Dominican Republic is its vibrant nightlife. By the time most visitors go home, their heads are ringing with the sounds of *merengue* and *bachata*, the two local forms of music that are inescapable, and irresistible to dance to.

Whether you stay in an all-inclusive resort or travel round the country independently, the one aspect of Dominican culture you can't avoid is the sound of *merengue* and *bachata* songs. They're on the radio and TV, in nightclubs and

– the *paseo*, or walk, in which couples take to the floor and begin to step to the beat; the *merengue* or melody itself; and finally the *jaleo*, a percussion-led, call-and-respond interaction between performer and

Dancin' in

bars throughout the country – often played at high volume – and they represent the joyful optimism of the Dominican people.

What is *Merengue*?

Merengue is a Latin rhythm that has just two basic beats to a bar, making it easy to dance to, but it includes syncopation (shifting stress to the weaker beat) and improvisation which allow musicians and dancers to go off on wild diversions during the performance. Each song has three basic phases

audience. Some couples maintain contact throughout a dance, while others like to do their own thing.

Obscure Origins

Just how the *merengue* originated is unclear. Some believe it came into being after independence

from Haiti in 1844, as one of the first known *merengue* songs is about a deserter in battle. Others suggest it was based on a musical form called *upa* from Cuba. Wherever it came from, it was frowned on by Dominican high society of the mid-19th century for its African rhythms, lascivious lyrics and suggestive, hip-swaying dance movements.

In those days however, most of the population lived in the countryside and *merengue* songs enjoyed great popularity. There were several regional variations, of which the *perico ripao* from Santiago became the most influential, perhaps because the Cibao Valley was then the main source of the country's wealth.

A Clever Election Ploy

Merengue continued to be marginalised by leaders of the DR until Rafael Trujillo swept to power in 1930. Though he ruthlessly eliminated opponents and rigged elections, he also knew that he needed to maintain popularity among the rural population, and so his supporters were treated to free *merengue* concerts by the big-name bands of the day. In 1936, he decreed *merengue* the official national music, and for the next 25 years Dominicans found themselves dancing to songs extolling the praises of *El*

the DR

Jefe. However, within months of his assassination, the top tune was *La Muerte del Chivo* (meaning "the death of the goat") (▶10).

Great *Merengueros*

The second half of the twentieth century brought about a revolution in global communications, and suddenly the DR was open to many outside musical influences, as well as making its own music famous abroad. Bandleaders **Johnny Ventura** and **Wilfrido Vargas** were the icons of *merengue* in the 70s and 80s, giving the horn

Top left: A musician practising the horn in a local store

Top: A flamboyant song and dance troupe at Carnival, Santo Domingo

Above: Tools of the trade, maracas

Left: Dancing the *merengue*

Merengue Festival on the Malecón

It's around 10 pm on a sultry night in late July and the Malecón in Santo Domingo is packed with people. The cars are moving slower than the pedestrians who flow in waves towards the open-air area where the annual Merengue Festival is taking place. The short approach to the concert area is crammed with stalls selling fried plantain, grilled pork and beef, soft drinks, beer and rum.

A crowd of excited locals and a few bewildered tourists throng in front of the stage, then surge forward when *Los Hermanos Rosario* (The Rosario Brothers), tonight's star act, appear on the stage. As the brothers launch into their performance, which includes some fantastically synchronised steps, everyone gets moving to the *merengue* beat. Most of the audience are in their 20s and 30s, but there are plenty of older folks and kids gyrating to the music too. Local girls move sinuously to the rhythm and there's no shortage of spruced up dudes hovering nearby, looking cool and hoping to attract their attention. Such scenes are repeated every night for two weeks, giving the capital its annual dose of *merengue* therapy.

sections a more prominent role and incorporating elements of soul, disco and funk. Yet the times were changing, and in the 1990s **Juan Luis Guerra** eclipsed the efforts of his seniors, not only as a great *merenguero*, but by popularising the long-discredited sound of *bachata*.

Bitter Songs Made Sweet

Like *merengue*, *bachata* (literally, "songs of bitterness") has been around a long time – as the folk music of the dispossessed, a kind of Dominican blues featuring a twangy guitar sound. Like *merengue* it was never accepted by the mainstream; that is, until Juan Luis Guerra recorded *Bachata Rosa* in the mid-1990s. Almost overnight, *bachata* went from being a socially unacceptable form of music to a fresh new sound drawing international acclaim. In the years that followed, musicians began fusing the two musical styles into a kind of *merenguechata* or *bachatarengue* that makes for great listening – a driving beat with high-pitched guitar picking and rousing vocals.

Dancers taking a well-deserved break

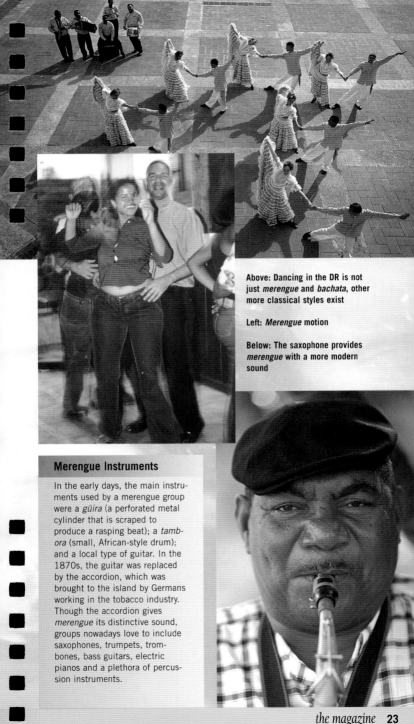

Above: Dancing in the DR is not just *merengue* and *bachata*, other more classical styles exist

Left: *Merengue* motion

Below: The saxophone provides *merengue* with a more modern sound

Merengue Instruments

In the early days, the main instruments used by a merengue group were a *güira* (a perforated metal cylinder that is scraped to produce a rasping beat); a *tambora* (small, African-style drum); and a local type of guitar. In the 1870s, the guitar was replaced by the accordion, which was brought to the island by Germans working in the tobacco industry. Though the accordion gives *merengue* its distinctive sound, groups nowadays love to include saxophones, trumpets, trombones, bass guitars, electric pianos and a plethora of percussion instruments.

La Cocina Dominicana

As with its people and music, the cuisine of the Dominican Republic draws on a wide range of influences, including Taíno, African and Spanish. The result is an exciting mixture of grains and pulses, meat and vegetables, usually spiced up with tasty sauces.

Eat the Flag

The most typical and most common dish in the DR is called **la bandera dominicana** (the Dominican flag). The red and white are represented by red beans and rice, and while there is no blue, it is a colourful and

nutritious dish, usually supplemented by fried plantain, chicken or pork stew and salad. Other Dominican favourites are **chivo guisado**, or goat stew, and **sancocho**, a soup made with at least five different kinds of meat, several tubers and plenty of vegetables. Two other popular dishes are **mofongo** and **mondongo**, the former being a mix of plantains, pork rinds and garlic and the latter a stew of tripe and entrails. Be careful not to mix them up if you have a weak stomach!

Above: Peppers and tomatoes, key ingredients in *La Cocina Dominicana*

Left: The DR's favourite beer, Presidente

Seafood and Chicken

As might be expected on a Caribbean island, the seafood is excellent and comes in a variety of preparations. Try the *camarones* (shrimps), *cangrejo* (crab), *mero* (sea bass) and for something a bit different, order the *lambi* (conch). Despite this great choice, nothing can compare in popularity with chicken in the DR, particularly fried chicken, and there are **pica pollo** outlets in even the smallest towns serving up the nation's favourite food.

Snacks

Dominicans love to snack at any time, and there are lots of tasty tidbits sold on the street that are well worth trying. One of the most common is the *pastelito*, which is a small envelope of pastry stuffed with meat or cheese. The meat stuffing is usually cooked with onions, tomatoes and olives, and sometimes mixed with chopped nuts and raisins, before being wrapped in its cover and fried. Very similar are *empanadas*, the wrapping of which is made of yucca flour.

Fruits and Drinks

One of the joys of being in a tropical country like the DR is the

fantastic *range of fruits* available. Apart from the ubiquitous favourites like coconuts, bananas, oranges and pineapples, there are many different kinds of mango and papaya as well as unusual items like *limoncillos*, small lime-shaped fruits with a refreshing pulp. As far as drinks are concerned, don't dare leave without trying at least one **batida** (fruit shake), a **Cuba libre** (rum and Coke), and a cup of local coffee.

Above: Freshly-squeezed orange juice, a tropical delight

Below: A beachside barbecue

Left: Mixed seafood platter

Amber

The Precious Resin

The Dominican Republic is one of the world's main sources of amber, a fossilised resin from the tree *Hymenaea Protera*, which became extinct around 25 million years ago. It is particularly prized for its honey or gold colour, yet Dominican amber also comes in shades of green, red and even blue, which is very rare. Dominican amber is reputed to be the best in the world for its range of colours, its translucency and high frequency of inclusions (small animals, insects or leaves trapped inside).

The amber mines in the DR are located at La Cumbre near the north coast in the Cordillera Septentrional, the mountain range between Santiago and Puerto Plata. The mines were part of the inspiration, as well as a setting for, the movie *Jurassic Park*, in which scientists managed to re-create dinosaurs from DNA found in the blood of a mosquito that had been trapped in amber. Astute observers have pointed out that while the amber in the movie was said to come from the Dominican Republic, the oldest amber in the country dates back only 25 million years, while dinosaurs became extinct around 65 million years ago.

The two amber museums in Santo Domingo (➤ 54) and Puerto Plata (➤ 71) are well worth visiting, both to find out how this precious resin is formed and to view some of the unusual pieces on display. These are the best places to buy a piece to take home, though amber is also on sale in jewellery shops and at souvenir stalls throughout the country. If you do plan to buy, take care as there is some very convincing plastic that looks identical.

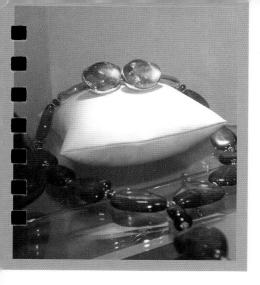

Left: A display of amber jewellery, Everett Designs, Altos de Chavón

Below: Dominican amber, the best in the world, is also the most beautiful

Facing page: Insects and other small animals can often be seen in amber

Fake or Real Amber?

Two common tests for amber are to put it in salt water or under a fluorescent lamp. Amber floats in brine whereas plastic sinks, and the glow of amber changes under fluorescent light, while that of plastic doesn't.

Baseball is far and away the most popular sport in the Dominican Republic, and since it was introduced in the late 19th century, its players have displayed great flair for the sport. The DR provides a whopping 10 per cent of all players in the North American League, including the legendary...

Slammin' Sammy

Pelota (ball), as the game is known in the DR, was first played on sugar cane plantations where owners provided a bat and ball to keep their workers happy. The American occupation of 1916–24 increased its popularity, and the first professional teams were formed. These days there are two teams in Santo Domingo and others in Santiago, San Pedro de Macorís and La Romana.

There are around 60 Dominican players in the US Major League and 500 or so in the Minor League, which is more than all other Latin American countries put together. Many of them, like Tony Peña, Pedro Martinez and Manny Ramirez, are household names in the USA, but the best performer of all is Slammin' Sammy Sosa. Born in Consuelo, near **San Pedro de Macorís**, Sammy used to sell orange juice and shine shoes to help his parents (and six brothers and sisters)

Left and above: Home run king, Sammy Sosa

to survive. In his spare time he played ball with his friends, using a milk carton as a glove, a rolled-up sock as a ball, and a broken branch as a bat. His big break came in 1989 when he was signed by the Texas Rangers, and reportedly he gave almost all of his first payment of $3,500 to his mother.

In 1992, Sosa was transferred to the Chicago Cubs, and though success was

Sosa

achievements, being frequently voted as Player of the Year in sports magazines, and even getting invites to the White House. Though now a multimillionaire and superstar, he hasn't forgotten his roots and the Sammy Sosa Foundation helps poor Dominican kids get a start in life. In every respect, Slammin' Sammy's life is the Dominican dream of rags-to-riches comes true.

not immediate, he was destined to become one of the greatest sluggers of all time. In 1998, along with Mark McGwire, he surpassed Roger Maris' record of 61 home runs in a season, which had stood for 37 years. Then in 1999 he hit over 60 again, the first player ever to do so in two seasons. The records keep on tumbling: in 2003 he notched up his 500th career home run, and is sure to hit many more before hanging up his bat. Not surprisingly, Sammy has received a lot of attention as a result of his

Above: Face for the future

Below: Baseball is still as popular as ever

DID YOU KNOW?

The word "rum" comes from *saccharum*, the Latin for sugar cane.

The game of polo was introduced to the DR in 1954 by Maharajah Jabar Singh, an Indian prince who was invited to teach Trujillo's sons. The sport is still played at Casa de Campo, and the season runs from November to mid-May.

People in the DR often call oranges *chinas* because the Chinese were the first to bring the plant here. (Spanish for orange is *naranja*)

There are over 50,000 hotel rooms to choose from in the DR.

There is also a small island in the Caribbean called "Dominica" whose people are also known as "Dominicans".

The Dominican Republic has both the highest and lowest points in the Caribbean — Pico Duarte at 3,087m (10,128ft), and Lago Enriquillo at almost 40m (130ft) below sea level.

After Santo Domingo, the city with the largest population of Dominicans is New York.

Playing dominoes and watching cock fighting are two of the most popular activities in the country.

The cannibalistic Caribs, who once terrorised the Taínos as well as European adventurers, had a particular penchant for Frenchmen, who they considered very tasty. English and Dutch were OK, but the Spanish they found stringy and inedible. In fact the word "cannibal" is derived from the flesh-eating Caribs.

The Dominican Republic is 48,730sq km (18,815sq miles) in area, a little larger than Holland, or half the size of the US State of Maine.

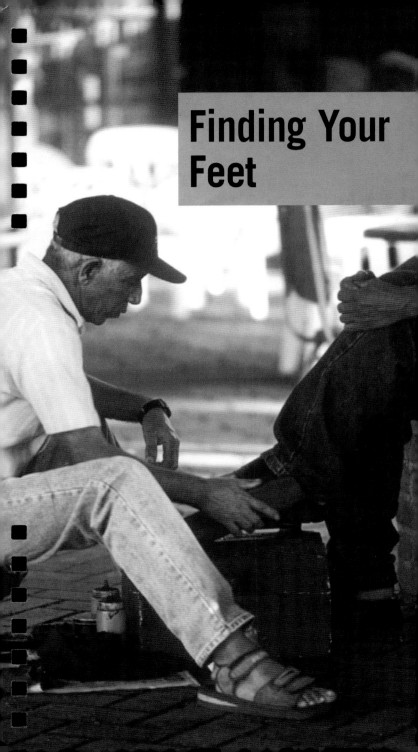

Finding Your Feet

First Two Hours

Arriving

There are eight **international airports** in the Dominican Republic – in Santo Domingo, Puerto Plata, Santiago, Punta Cana, La Romana, Barahona and Samaná, though at the time of writing the last two were not receiving international flights. The main reason for having so many international airports in such a small country is to be able to deal with tourists staying at the all-inclusive resorts. So if you are booked in an all-inclusive resort at Bávaro, your charter flight will arrive in Punta Cana and a resort representative will meet you and escort you on the short trip by minibus to your base. In this way all visitors on pre-paid holidays are virtually guaranteed a smooth landing.

If you are not on a pre-paid holiday, chances are you will arrive at **Aeropuerto Internacional Las Américas** (549 0081/89) about 30km (19 miles) east of Santo Domingo. It's a 35 minute taxi trip into town. Unless someone is meeting you, there's no other easy way of getting into Santo Domingo.

Aeropuerto Internacional Las Américas

■ Be prepared for long queues at **immigration** if a number of flights arrive simultaneously.
■ **Complete the form** that you were given on the flight and hand it to the immigration official.
■ There is a **currency exchange** booth and **cash dispenser** machine beyond customs, as well as **car rental agencies**.
■ Brace yourself to be assailed by **cab drivers** and **tour guides** if you are not being picked up.
■ The standard cab fare from the airport to the centre of Santo Domingo is US$20 and the trip takes around half an hour. **Negotiate the fare before** setting out as cab drivers don't use meters.
■ The **taxi drivers** make sure that no buses link the airport with downtown Santo Domingo. If the fare seems too steep, find someone in the taxi queue to share.

Tourist Information Offices

Santo Domingo There are two tourist information offices in Santa Domingo. The main office is the Secretariá de Estado de Turismo at Oficinas Gubernmentales, Bloque D, Avenida México and 30 de Marzo (tel: 221 4660; fax: 682-3806; www.dominicana.com.do; weekdays, 9-5). There's also a branch office at: Palacio Borghella, Calle Isabela la Catolica, Parque Colón (tel: 686 3858; daily 9–5)
Barahona Carreterra Batey Central, (tel: 524 3650)
Cabarete Autopista Principal de Cabarete (tel: 571 0962)
La Romana Edificio de la Gobernación (tel: 550 6922, 550 3242)
La Vega Calle Melta Esq. Duvegé, Edificio de la Gobernación (tel: 242 3231, 573 7678)
Puerto Plata Avenida Hermanas Mirabal #1, Parque Costero (tel: 586 3676, 320 0901)
Samaná Avenida Santa barbara, Edificio Oficinas Pública (tel: 538 2332)
San Pedro de Macorís Calle Ramón Montalvo #10, (tel: 529 3644)
Santiago Calle Juan Pablo Duarte #85, Palacio Municipal (tel: 582 5885)
Sosúa Calle Sosúa–Cabarete, Edificio Gel Brown (tel: 571 3433)

Getting Around

The Dominican Republic has domestic flights from Santo Domingo to most major towns, and all flights last less than an hour. Car hire is easy to arrange, and buses run regularly and efficiently between main towns. For getting around on the beach, rent a motorbike or quad (4WD motorbike), but to savour the fresh air of the Cordillera, hire a horse. In most city centres, including Santo Domingo, walking is the way to go.

Domestic Flights

Air Santo Domingo (tel: 683 8006, fax: 381 0080, www.air-santodomingo.com) operates regular flights connecting Santo Domingo with Puerto Plata, Santiago, Punta Cana, La Romana, El Portillo (near Las Terrenas) and Arroyo Barríl (near Samaná). Prices range between US$50–100 for tickets.

- Caribair (tel: 542 6688, www.caribintair.com) operates flights to Barahona in the southwest, as well as to Port-au-Prince in Haiti.
- Domestic flights leave from **Aeropuerto Internacional Herrera**, which is about a US$10 ride from downtown by cab. A new domestic airport, Aeropuerto La Isabela, was also due to open at the time of press.

Car and Motorbike Hire

- You must be at least **25 years old** and have a valid **driver's licence** and a **credit card** to hire a car or motorbike in the DR.
- Daily rates begin at around US$50 for a car (US$70 for 4WD) and US$20 for a motorbike. It is often cheaper to **book in advance** with an international car rental company.
- International **car rental** companies like Avis, Hertz and Budget all have offices at the airport and in downtown Santo Domingo.
    AVIS: Avenida Abraham Lincoln (tel: 535 7191)
    Budget: Avenida JF Kennedy (tel: 566 6666)
    National: Avenida Abraham Lincoln (tel: 562 1444)
- **Motorbikes** are only available in places geared to independent travellers, such as Cabarete and Las Terrenas.

Driving

Driving in the DR is a very different experience to driving in Europe or the USA in that trucks, cars and buses are constantly overtaking and forcing other vehicles off the road. A foreigner involved in an accident is likely to be held responsible whatever the circumstances. You must be prepared to adapt your road manners and drive cautiously.

- If you are confident about driving in this brave new world, a hired vehicle gives you maximum freedom to go where you want, when you want. Since the DR is not too big, you are always within a few hours drive of anywhere on the island. **4WD vehicles** are ideal for getting off the beaten track.
- Drive on the **right side** of the road.
- **Speed limits** are either 80 or 100 kph (50 or 63 mph) on main highways, and 40–60 kph (25–37 mph) in built-up areas.
- Wearing **seat belts** is compulsory by law, but attitudes towards this are lax.
- Although there are few traffic police, fines for **traffic violations** are usually US$10.
- Though the roads leading north, east and west of Santo Domingo are in **good condition**, be prepared for potholes on other country roads.

- The authorities have installed massive traffic speed bumps across some roads that would destroy any vehicle approaching at faster than 8kph (5mph). Look out for these at the approach to each village and town in the countryside, and also **keep an eye open** for the opposite – ditches dug across the road which slow vehicles down to a crawl.
- At present there are **no drinking and driving laws** in the DR.

Taxis

Taxis are easy to find around the major towns (they all have signs stating "Taxi" on the roofs), but you must agree on the fare before starting, as **drivers don't use meters**. Companies generally post their rates to common destinations outside their offices. A reliable company in Santo Domingo is Maxi Taxi (tel: 544 0077).

Buses

The bus network is very extensive, connecting all towns of any size in the DR and is the least expensive option for the independent traveller.

- Two reliable companies, **Caribe Tours** (tel: 221 4422, www.caribetours.com.do) and **Metro Bus** (tel: 566 7126), offer connections between major towns in the country.
- To get off the beaten track, you'll need to wave down a *guagua* (pronounced "wa-wa"), which are battered vans that serve as local buses and are constantly overcrowded. A little Spanish can go a long way in these gregarious vehicles, but as long as you state your destination clearly, it isn't absolutely necessary.

Quads and Horses

If you stay somewhere geared up for independent travellers such as Las Terrenas, you can hire a **quad** (4WD motorbike) to go exploring the nearby countryside. With their large wheels and compact size, these things can go almost anywhere, but be careful not to trespass on private property. If you prefer a more traditional form of transport, hire a **horse** for a romantic ride along the beach, or for a challenging trek into the hills.

Guided Tours

Many of the country's top attractions, like **whale watching** in Bahía de Samaná (➤ 90), **white-water rafting** on the Río Yaque del Norte (➤ 148) and **snorkelling** at offshore islands like Isla Saona (➤ 114), are found on the itineraries of tour companies. They will pick you up at your hotel, take you maybe halfway across the island, and lay on a great day with lunch included. Such tours don't come cheap, but they do make it possible to fit in a lot during a short stay. Some reliable operators are:

Maxima Aventura, Rancho Baiguate, Jarabacoa (tel: 574 6890, www.ranchobaiguate.com)
Iguana Mama, Cabarete, 571 0908, 800-849-4720 toll free from USA, fax 571 0734, www.iguanamama.com)
Outback Safari, Plaza Turisol, Local 7, Avenida Luperon Km 2.5, Puerto Plata (tel: 244 4886, www.outbacksafari.com.do)

Admission Charges
The price of admission to places mentioned in this guide is represented by the following categories:
Inexpensive under US$1   **Moderate** US$1–2   **Expensive** over US$2

Accommodation

The Dominican Republic has plenty of accommodation for visitors, – over 50,000 hotel rooms at the last count. Most of these are located in the huge, all-inclusive resorts, but there are plenty of alternatives for those who would rather go it alone. Luxury, mid-range and budget hotels can be found in all main towns, offering a variety of facilities. Bear in mind when looking at hotel rates that a hefty 22 per cent tax will be added to your bill (this comprises a 10 per cent service charge and 12 per cent government tax).

All-Inclusive Resorts

- The all-inclusive system is simple – you pay a fixed price to your local travel agent for a return flight and a week or two in a resort. This includes a room (**usually very comfortable**, with facilities such as cable TV), all the food and drink you want in the buffet, restaurants and bars, plus a variety of beach and water activities and evening entertainment.
- Rates in Dominican all-inclusives are the **most competitive** in the entire Caribbean. In the low season (May–November), a package holiday costs only a little more than the normal price of a return plane fare, so it's not surprising that around 80 per cent of tourists arriving in the DR choose this option.
- Most resorts cover hundreds of acres of **landscaped grounds** with various bars and restaurants, swimming pools, gymnasiums, tennis courts and other sports facilities.
- The major concentrations of all-inclusives are around Punta Cana and Bávaro on the east coast and Playa Dorada on the north coast. However, some are located in **more isolated spots** like the southwest.
- The great strength of the all-inclusives is that they allow you to **relax completely**. Once guests have been tagged with a coloured wristband at reception, they are free to use all the facilities within the resort's walls.
- The resorts have their drawbacks, however. Their massive size makes them rather impersonal, and the high walls around add to a sense of unreality within. Guests learn little about Dominican culture except how to wiggle to a *merengue* beat, and many see nothing of the country's wonderful landscapes or historical sites unless they sign up for a pricey **day trip** from the resort.

Luxury Hotels

There are lots of top-class hotels in the DR, ranging from towering monoliths to quaint colonial buildings. Several are run by international chains, such as Renaissance, Melia and Sofitel, and most are found in Santo Domingo, though there is usually at least one in every other major city and coastal resort. The standard of facilities and services is very high, and most reduce their rates in the low season. Expect air-conditioning, mini-bars, cable TV, maid service, at least two or three bars and restaurants, swimming pools and sometimes a business centre.

Mid-range Hotels

There are plenty of smaller hotels in the DR where service is more personal and guests can choose from a variety of rooms to suit their pocket. The more expensive rooms may be quite spacious, with mini-bar and cable TV, and though cheaper rooms may be smaller and more spartan, they enjoy the same level of service and can often be very good value.

Budget Hotels

There is not much budget accommodation in the DR, and that which exists is poorly lacking in facilities and services – it usually entails **a cramped room** with no view and sharing bathrooms with no hot water. Remember, too, that the DR is in the tropics. With no air-conditioning and restricted windows the nights can be long and uncomfortably hot. There are exceptions to the rule, however, and in destinations popular with independent travellers such as Las Terrenas and Cabarete, it is possible to find attractive rooms with reasonable facilities for around US$30 per night.

Pensions

Small "bed and breakfast" style pensions are becoming increasingly common in the DR and are popular with visitors who want to meet the locals. Much more personal than a hotel, they are generally private houses whose owners have decided to supplement their income by taking in paying guests. Most pensions serve meals as part of the deal, and if you choose to stay in one you're likely to spend time talking with the owner(s) over dinner and quite possibly again over breakfast. If you don't mind – or even seek – this level of intimacy with Dominicans, then staying at a pension can be **an economically appealing opportunity**.

Camping

Though Dominicans occasionally like to camp out rough on a beach or in the hills, there are **no official campsites** equipped with basic facilities, except in the national parks, and even here facilities are basic. If you sign up for a trek of several days, the company will provide camping equipment, so it is hardly worth taking a tent with you on your travels. Officially approved camping sites exist in the Parque Nacional Armando Bermúdez and Parque Nacional José del Carmen Ramírez. Note, however, that facilities here are **primitive at best**. In general the DR should be considered unsuitable for camping, not least because the Dominicans tend to look askance at foreign visitors sleeping out in tents in the open. By definition, visitors are rich, and such behaviour is inexplicable to the locals.

High Season and Low Season

Hotel rates, particularly in the all-inclusives, vary wildly according to the season. The **high season** lasts from **December until April**, and many places are fully booked for New Year and Easter, when Dominicans typically take a holiday themselves. The **low season** runs from **May to November**, during which time prices plummet by 30–40 per cent and there are some great deals to be had.

Advance Booking

To get a good rate at the all-inclusives, it is necessary to book well in advance from your own country. Before visiting your travel agent, check out the websites of resorts that appeal to find out what is on offer. Though some of these resorts will accept walk-in guests or day visitors, the rates are much higher. There is no need to book ahead for other hotels unless your visit coincides with a major holiday or festival (➤ 11).

Prices
For a typical double room per night, excluding 22 per cent tax
(10 per cent service charge, 12 per cent government tax)
$ under US$50   **$$** US$50–100   **$$$** over US$100

Food and Drink

Along with dancing to *merengue* music, eating and drinking are favourite activities for Dominicans, so visitors to the country generally have no problem finding good places to eat and drink. All the major towns frequented by tourists have a range of international restaurants – with Italian, Spanish, Mexican, French, Chinese and even British cuisine – as well as local food on the menu.

Where to Eat

Options range from munching on snacks at streetside stalls to truly elegant dining with starched linen and silverware. At the basic level are *comedores* (simple restaurants), which are usually clean and cheap and offer a limited range of daily specials. All the cities and resort towns have a choice of fancy restaurants, where the menus offer a range of international dishes. If you are staying in an all-inclusive resort, your options are the buffet for any meal and restricted use (usually once a week) of whatever á la carte restaurants are available. Beyond this there are simple cafés and wandering vendors selling all kinds of fare on many beaches, while picnics make an attractive option on tours.

Main Dishes

Dominican *comida criolla*, or local food, fuses many elements such as rice, beans and meat to produce dishes like *la bandera dominicana*, *sancocho* and *chivo guisado* (➤ 24). Spices are used to great effect, though the use of chilli is sparing and no dishes are likely to sting your tongue. In general, *comida criolla* presents a good nutritional balance, but many dishes are fried and you may find them too greasy.

Desserts and Drinks

There is a wide range of desserts in the DR, although some are too sweet for many visitors. Some worth trying are *dulces con coco*, which are made of molasses and grated coconut, *dulces con leche*, which contain sweetened curdled milk, and *flan de maíz*, a corn custard similar to a creme caramel. A healthier alternative is a plate of fresh tropical fruit. Dominican drinks are simply irresistible, from thirst-quenching fruit shakes to mind-mellowing rum and eye-opening coffee.

When to Eat

One aspect of Spanish culture that has stuck is the habit of eating a late lunch, followed by a siesta, and taking a late dinner too; it is not unusual for Dominicans to eat **lunch at 2 pm** and **dinner at 9 pm**. Unusually, **Monday night** is the big night of the week for many Dominicans, so don't be surprised to find restaurants busier then.

Menus, Tipping and Dress Codes

Most restaurants in tourist areas have menus in both Spanish and English. However, there are lots of excellent *comedores*, or eating rooms, that serve up great food at reasonable prices but only have Spanish menus, so it's certainly worth learning some food vocabulary. Ten per cent Service is included in the bills, but an additional 10 per cent tip would be considered courteous. As befits such a laid-back country, there is no particular dress code in most restaurants, though all-inclusive resorts do not permit guests to enter the buffet in swimwear.

Shopping

The Dominican Republic has plenty to interest shoppers. Some of what is on offer is tacky, but it's also possible to pick up a unique piece of amber or larimar, a classic Caribbean painting, aromatic cigars and smooth-tasting rum, as well as CDs of the DR's very own music, *merengue* and *bachata*.

What to Buy

- **Amber and larimar** (➤ 26) make ideal souvenirs of this magical land that produces substances of such gorgeous hues. Large pieces can run to tens of thousands of dollars, but a small pendant or ring set with a piece of either stone can be gratifyingly affordable.

- **Paintings**, by both Dominican and Haitian artists, are available all over the DR and a perfect way to liven up your living room. Executed in bright colours and bold designs, they range from small reproductions to huge, original canvases. Even if a canvas is large, getting it home isn't really a problem. Galleries will be pleased to remove it from its frame and roll it into a specially made canister for transportation. Watch out for attractive wood and stone carvings from both the DR and neighbouring Haiti at art galleries throughout the island.

- **Old Spanish coins**, particularly the famous "Pieces of Eight" long associated with the era of pirates, galleons and the Spanish Main, make excellent and unusual souvenirs. They are available at around US$100 at the Museo de las Atarazanas (➤ 51) on Calle las Atarazanas in Santo Domingo. Their sale is legal and their export permitted.

- **Cigars and rum** (➤ 18) are surefire hits as presents for smoking or drinking friends. Dominican cigars are rated alongside those from Cuba, while the various types of rum offer a true taste of the DR's exotic side.

- **CDs** of *merengue* and *bachata* music (➤ 20) are also a perfect way to bring memories of a stay flooding back. Buy a few copies of a recent compilation of the country's hits, and hand them out to your best friends. There's no better way to show the irrepressible joy of the country.

- You would be well advised to steer clear of products made of turtle shell, black coral and mahogany as these are all **endangered species**. Other dubious purchases which might land visitors in trouble with either the DR authorities or their home customs include products manufactured from the American crocodile, giant conch shells and many plant species, notably endemic orchids which are protected by DR and international laws.

Where to Buy

As a country geared up for tourism, typical Dominican souvenirs are available in all areas frequented by visitors, but the range and quality of products can vary considerably. Santo Domingo has by far the widest range and best quality, especially at Calle El Conde and Mercado Modelo. Visits to the cigar and rum factories in Santiago and Puerto Plata also present good opportunities to stock up on gifts.

Opening Hours and Credit Cards

Regular opening hours for shops are from 8:30 am–6:30 pm, with a two-hour lunch break from 12 noon until 2 pm, though places selling souvenirs in or around hotels and resorts tend to stay open much later, in some cases till 10 or 11 pm. Most places accept major credit cards, but it's always useful to have a fistful of dollars in your pocket in case.

Entertainment

Dominicans are a fun-loving people, and jump at any opportunity to have a good time. Apart from a full festival calendar (➤ 11), there are frequent concerts of live music and cinemas showing the latest films. Sports feature in a big way in the DR too, with lots of beach activities like windsurfing and snorkelling, as well as top-class golf courses. As for spectator sports, baseball is by far the most popular.

Events Information

■ For information about upcoming events, pick up a copy of the major national newspaper, **Listin Diario**, or the **Diario Libre**, which is available in many shopping outlets in the Zona Colonial. A useful - website for information about entertainment in the capital is www.aquisantodomingo.com

■ Of course the **Tourist Information offices** can provide you with details and ideas of things to do. For addresses of these offices see the First Two Hours section (➤ 32).

Festivals

■ All the major Christian festivals are celebrated in a big way in the DR, particularly **Samana Santa** – Easter – which involves grand parades in many towns.

■ If you are considering visiting in **February** or **July**, make an effort to be there for Carnival or the **Merengue Festival** (➤ 12), when an exciting atmosphere prevails.

■ While travelling around the country, ask about the local *fiesta patronal* (patron saint's day festival), when you can witness African drumming and dancing fused alongside Christian piety.

Live Music and Nightclubs

■ The local music, *merengue* and *bachata*, is great to listen to and dance to, and all over the island, particularly in Santo Domingo, there are frequent performances by local groups. Good venues for live music in Santo Domingo are the Guácara Taíno and the Merengue Bar in the Renaissance Jaragua Hotel (➤ 60) Check the "**Where to be entertained**" sections of the guide for more details.

■ There are **nightclubs** in many all-inclusive resorts, lots of large hotels and all main town centres. Mostly they play eminently danceable *merengue* and *bachata*, but where tourists gather, they are likely to inject the mix with music that is more familiar to the visitors. A couple of lively clubs in the provinces are La Barrica in Puerto Plata (➤ 82) and Nuevo Mundo in Las Terrenas (➤ 100).

■ Most nightclubs don't open until 10 or 11 pm, and **few people arrive before midnight**.

Cinemas

Most major towns have cinemas that show up-to-date films, though the majority of them are dubbed in Spanish. Call to check if they have an English soundtrack – this is more likely at some of the up-market cinemas in Santo Domingo and other large cities. All-inclusive resorts and bars catering mainly to overseas visitors regularly show videos or DVDs in English for the entertainment of their guests.

Classical Concerts

There are occasional performances by the National Symphony Orchestra, as well as ballet and opera, at the Teatro Nacional in Santo Domingo at 35 Avenida Maximo Gomez (tel: 687 3191).

Entertainment at All-inclusive Resorts

The all-inclusive resorts make a big effort to ensure their guests have plenty of activities to choose from, both in the day and at night. Daytime activities include aerobics in and around the pool, *merengue* dance lessons, beach volleyball and football, windsurfing instruction, etc. In some places you can learn to dive and go home with an internationally recognised diving certificate. At night most all-inclusives will put on elaborate shows featuring the music, song and dance of the Dominican Republic (and elsewhere). Audience participation is encouraged. Discos are commonplace and very popular.

Organised Tours and Theme Parks

If you get restless being in the same environment at an all-inclusive, sign up at reception for one of the many organised tours that will take you on a sightseeing trip around the capital, a visit to cigar and rum factories, an offshore snorkelling trip, or many other activities. Most children would enjoy a visit to a theme park like Manati Park in Bávaro (➤ 118) or Ocean World near Puerto Plata.

Sports

Baseball is the DR's most popular sport, and if you are in the country during the season (mid-Nov–mid-Feb), it's certainly worth going along to a game to witness the passion that it arouses in the spectators. In Santo Domingo, the Estadio Quisqueya at the corner of Maximo Gomez and Kennedy (tel: 565 5565) is the place to go.

The DR is a **golfer's paradise**, partly due to the idyllic climate. Even in the rainy season, showers tend to be brief, and many people come here principally for a golfing holiday. There are courses located in all parts of the island, some designed by internationally renowned architects like Pete Dye and Robert Trent Jones. Several of those near the coast have fantastic views out over either the Atlantic or the Caribbean. A few of the very best are:

Santo Domingo Country Club, Calle Isabel Aguilar (tel: 530 6606);
Guavaberry Golf & Country Club, Autovia del Este, Juan Dolio, San Pedro de Macorís (tel: 526 2424);
The Teeth of the Dog, Casa de Campo, La Romana (tel: 523 8115);
Punta Cana Golf Club, Punta Cana (tel: 959 4653);
Playa Grande Golf Course, Km 9, Carretera Rio San Juan – Cabarete (tel: 582 0860).

■ The fantastic beaches that surround the DR offer plenty of opportunities for **watersports**. Learn the tricky techniques of kitesurfing and windsurfing; go snorkelling or diving around coral reefs; join a deep-sea fishing trip or just enjoy sailing round the bay.

■ In the hills near Jarabacoa, **white-water rafting** trips along the Río Yaque del Norte (➤ 148) are an exhilarating and very popular way to spend a day.

■ Jarabacoa (➤ 147) is also the DR's centre for **adventure sports**, which include horseback riding, mountain biking, or canyoning down a river valley. The fresh climate of the Cordillera Central also makes the region ideal for hiking, and the ultimate challenge to hikers is to climb Pico Duarte, the highest point in the Caribbean.

Santo Domingo

Getting Your Bearings

In 1498, Santo Domingo became the first city to be established by Europeans in the Americas, and is currently the fastest-growing city in the Caribbean. The magnetic attraction for visitors is the Zona Colonial (Colonial Zone), where hundreds of historic buildings are clustered in a compact area convenient for exploring on foot.

13 Jardín Botánico

AVENIDA MEXICO

Mercado Modelo **8**

AVENIDA 30 DE MARZO

Museo de Arte Moderno **12**

Parque Independencia **9**

AVENIDA BOLIVAR

ENRIQUE HENRIQUEZ

AVENIDA INDEPENDENCIA

5 Malecón

AV GEORGE WASHINGTON (MALECÓN)

★ Don't Miss

1 Catedral de Santa María la Menor ➤ 46
2 Calle de las Damas ➤ 48
3 Plaza España ➤ 50
4 Calle El Conde ➤ 52
5 Malecón ➤ 53

Previous page: Santo Domingo's carnival celebrations are always colourful and usually highly imaginative
Left: Christopher Columbus statue, Parque Colón, Zona Colonial

At Your Leisure

0 ————— 400 metres
0 ————— 400 yards

Faro a Colón
14

3 Plaza España

AV MELLA

DUARTE MACORIS

Hospital de
San Nicolás
de Bari
10

ARZ MERINO

AV ESPAÑA

AV. ESTADOS UNIDOS

6 Museo de Ámbar

1 Catedral de Santa
María la Menor

4 TELERA

EL CONDE

HOSTOS

ARZ NOUEL

ARZ NOUELOS

7

2 Calle de las Damas

4
Calle
El Conde

11

Museo de Larimar

Convento
de los
Dominicos

*Puerto
Ozama*

15

AV ESPAÑA

Acuario
Nacional

Right in the heart of the Zona Colonial,
the Catedral de Santa María la Menor is
the most important building in the
country and a good spot to begin and
end a stroll around the city. In the
nearby Calle de las Damas (Street of the
Ladies) and Plaza España, you can visit
places like the Museo de Las Casas
Reales (Museum of the Royal Houses),
the Alcázar de Colón (Palace of
Columbus), and immerse yourself in
the world of five centuries ago. The
Calle El Conde (Street of the Count) is
a good place to buy souvenirs of your
stay. In the evening, the Malecón is the
place to go to join locals dancing to
merengue in one of the seafront bars or
in one of the nightclubs in the big
hotels that look out over the Caribbean.

**At the Plaza de la Cultura,
Museo del Hombre
Dominicano**

Santo Domingo in Two Days

Day One

Morning

Start in Parque Colón (below), in the heart of the Zona Colonial, where a statue of Christopher Columbus is the central feature. First stop should be the awe-inspiring and serene **🔒Catedral de Santa María la Menor** (➤ 46). Before leaving the square, take a look around the **🔟Museo de Ámbar** (➤ 54).

Go round the corner to the **🔟Museo de Larimar** (➤ 54) and compare the pale blue stone that is unique to this island. From here, head east across to **🔟Calle de las Damas** (➤ 48). Stroll north along this quaint colonial street to the **🔟Plaza España** (➤ 50).

Afternoon

Treat yourself to a long, slow lunch at any one of a string of restaurants around the west side of Plaza España (below); a good lunch buffet can be found at La Atarazana (➤ 61). Cross to the east side of Plaza España for a look at the **Alcázar de Colón** (➤ 50), former palace of Diego Columbus, Christopher's son. Then go on to the **Museo de las Atarazanas** (➤ 51) and gaze on booty salvaged from sunken galleons.

Evening

For dinner, check out one of the city's many gourmet restaurants, such as Paparazzo (➤ 62), then dance off any excess weight at one of the nightclubs situated along the seafront **5 Malecón** (➤ 53).

Day Two

Morning

Begin in Parque Colón again, but this time head west along **4 Calle El Conde** (➤ 52). Browsing the windows and shopping for souvenirs such as *merengue* CDs, makes for great reminders of your stay. If you are hungry, grab a bite in one of the many cafés along the street. When you reach the Puerta del Conde, go through the arch and take a short break in the **9 Parque Independencia** (➤ 55).

Afternoon

There are plenty of options from here, depending on your taste. For more shopping, stroll northeast on Avenida Mella to the **8 Mercado Modelo** (➤ 55). Or, learn a little about Dominican culture by hopping into a cab and heading further west to the Plaza de la Cultura. In this square you will find the **12 Museo de Arte Moderno** (➤ 57) and other museums dedicated to the history, geography and natural history of the country. Alternatively, follow the short walk around the Zona Colonial (➤ 158) for a look at the ruins of the **10 Hospital de San Nicolás de Bari** (➤ 56)and the honey-coloured bricks of the **11 Convento de los Dominicos** (➤ 56).

Evening

Head for Calle Hostos, where you will find Aljibe Café (➤ 61), which serves tasty and filling meals, and later in the evening transforms into a funky nightclub with live music and dancing.

Catedral de Santa María la Menor

This was the first cathedral to be built in all the Americas, and was therefore the base for the spread of Christianity across the continent. In its early days it hosted animated parades by African slaves and was ransacked by Sir Francis Drake, but these days a hushed aura of reverence prevails.

Diego Columbus, Christopher's son, laid the first stone for the cathedral in 1514, but work did not begin in earnest until 1521 when the first bishop arrived. It was completed in 1541 and was granted the status of cathedral by Pope Paul III in 1546. In its early days, it was attended not only by Christians but also by African slaves for their patron saint parades, until the clergy saw the "subversive", frenzied dancing and drumming that accompanied such parades, and quickly banished such practices from this hallowed ground.

Visitors enter through the north door from Parque Colón and are immediately confronted by an unusual mix of Gothic, Spanish Renaissance and baroque architecture, which somehow blends into a pleasing fusion. Even the stained glass windows, though modern in

The belltower of Catedral de Santa María la Menor

design, are based on ancient method. The Gothic, vaulted ceiling is a delight to look at, and there are altars of marble and mahogany.

Fourteen chapels line the north and south walls, some of which are blessed with macabre names. The Chapel of Life and Death has an intriguing window depicting a beard-less Jesus being baptised by a wild-looking John the Baptist; whereas the Chapel of Christ in Agony is guarded by two stone lions who preside over the grave of Santo Domingo's first bishop, Alejandro Geraldini. The remains of Christopher Columbus are said to have been interred in the Chapel of the Virgin of the Light until they were trans-ferred to the Faro a Colón in 1992, on the occasion of the 500th anniversary of his arrival in the Americas. However, since other countries claim possession of Columbus' remains, the truth of the matter is currently unclear (➤ 55).

The best exterior view of the cathedral is from the west side, where a frieze of cherubs is carved above the high-arched doorways, and intricate carvings of famous priests flank them. On the outside of the western gates (usually closed) are metal carvings of some highly individual and expressive heads.

One unusual sight from the west side of the cathedral is an unprotected bell tower. This is part of the legacy of Sir Francis Drake, who used the cathedral as a barracks when he attacked and plundered the city in 1586 (➤ 17). He stripped off the bell tower's cover and stole anything of value he could find, including a gold Hapsburg seal and several statues.

A finely sculpted statue at the cathedral's western entrance

TAKING A BREAK

El Conde (➤ 61), in the northwest corner of Parque Colón, offers a good range of meals and drinks at reasonable prices. It's also an ideal spot for people-watching from tables that spill on to the square.

➕ 185 D4 ✉ Parque Colón 🕐 Daily 9–4 🎫 Free

CATEDRAL DE SANTA MARÍA LA MENOR: INSIDE INFO

Top tips Visitors are not allowed to enter the cathedral or other religious sites in shorts or sleeveless shirts, or trousers for women, so **dress respectfully** in such places.

• As the city's major sight, the cathedral can get crowded with tour groups. To **avoid the crowds**, go early or late in the day.

② Calle de las Damas

Running parallel to the Ozama River, this was the first street to be laid by Nicolás de Ovando when he moved the town from the east bank of the river in 1502. Thus it claims to be the oldest street in the Western Hemisphere, and it acquired its name from the ladies who used to walk up and down it in attendance to the wife of Diego Columbus.

The southern end of the street is dominated by the battlement walls of the **Fortaleza Ozama** (Fort Ozama), which was the point where Spanish conquests of countries like Cuba, Jamaica and Colombia began. It also fulfilled the vital role of protecting the city from invaders – who invariably came from the sea – until it was decommissioned in the 1960s. The most prominent building within its grounds, and the only one open to visitors, is the **Torre del Homenaje** (Tower of Homage), which was formerly a prison. It is also possible to climb 18m (60 feet) to the top for a panoramic view of the Zona Colonial.

There are many beautifully-preserved buildings along this street, including the Casa de Francia, built in 1503 and where conquistador, Hernan Cortez is said to have dreamt up his plan to invade the New World. These days it is home to the cultural division of the French Embassy, which occasionally hosts art exhibitions. Also striking is the Panteón Nacional (National Mausoleum), a sombre, neoclassical memorial to the country's military and political heroes, with a stern-looking guard on permanent duty.

Fortaleza Ozama dominates Santo Domingo's harbour

However, the edifice of most interest to visitors is the **Museo de las Casas Reales** (Museum of the Royal Houses). It features colonial relics from the 16th–18th centuries, such as weapons, wine bottles and coins, as well as a map charting the voyages of Christopher Columbus.

Fortaleza Ozama; the Spanish planned their conquest of the Caribbean from the fort

The building itself dates from the 16th century and has now been restored to its former grandeur, when it functioned as the administrative centre for Spanish interests in the West Indies. In front of the building is a sundial, erected in 1752 and positioned so that bureaucrats could tell the time from the window of their office.

TAKING A BREAK

There are no restaurants or cafés on the street itself, but plenty of options in nearby streets, especially around Plaza España. Why not try some Spanish tapas at **Museo de Jamón**? (➤ 62)

Fortaleza Ozama
✚ 185 E4
🕐 Daily 9–7 💲 Inexpensive

Casa de Francia
✚ 185 E4
🕐 Mon–Fri 9–4:30 💲 Free

Panteón Nacional
✚ 185 E4
🕐 Mon–Sat 9–7 💲 Free

Museo de las Casas Reales
✚ 185 E4
🕐 Tue–Sun 9–6 💲 Inexpensive

CALLE DE LAS DAMAS: INSIDE INFO

Top tip Resist the **temptation to wander round every colonial building** on this street, or you will never get to see the rest of the city.

Hidden gem Keep your eyes open for **five disfigured gargoyles** leering down from above the door to the Casa de las Gárgolas, just two houses away from the Panteón Nacional. Their battered condition is caused not only by the ravages of time, but also by a stoning from a mob that held them responsible for some suspicious murders in the 17th century.

3 Plaza España

Plaza España is a large open area surrounded by old city walls, colonial buildings and restaurants. Located right next to the port, this was once the busiest part of the city, with officials coming and going to their posts, sailors enjoying time off and merchants selling slaves. Fortunately things are a bit quieter these days, and you should be able to stroll around it at leisure. The old city walls and the Puerta San Diego offer a nostalgic aura of medieval Europe to the plaza.

The Moorish arches of the Alcázar de Colón

In the northeast corner of the square, the Moorish arches of the **Alcázar de Colón** show the Islamic influence in Spanish architecture during the colonial era. This is another of the Zona Colonial's most important buildings, having been con-structed from coral stone by Diego Columbus between 1511 and 1515, without using a single nail. Diego had already succeeded Nicolás de Ovando as governor in 1509 in recognition of his father's great discovery. He chose this location for his base because of its proximity to both the **Casas Reales** (▶ 49), which he visited frequently, and the docks, over which it looks out. He lived here until 1523, when he was recalled to Spain, but was succeeded by other favoured names of the Spanish Court such as Pizarro, Cortez and Ponce de León.

These days the interior has been refurbished and functions as a museum, displaying furniture, tapestries, silverware and gargoyles from the early 16th century. A stone staircase leads upstairs to a collection of illuminated manuscripts from the period as well as a harp and a clavichord in the music room.

There are also good **photo opportunities** of the river and the plaza from the upper floor.

Just north of the Alcázar, down a few steps, is the narrow street called Las Atarazanas (The Docks). Taverns and restaurants, once hosts to medieval sailors, now cater to tourists. The largest building, right in front of the Puerta las Atarazanas (Docks Gate) is the **Museo de las Atarazanas** (Docks Museum), which offers a good idea of life on board a 16th century ship. The display recounts the numerous efforts to salvage the treasures from ships that sank offshore, and includes cannons, swords, crucifixes, silver and crystal.

Las Atarazanas street forms a curve around the west side of Plaza España. It contains many of the city's most popular restaurants, where customers sit and look out over the plaza, and are usually entertained by live musicians in the evening.

TAKING A BREAK

If you're here around lunchtime, **La Atarazana** (➤ 61) serves up an excellent buffet in a restful ambience, while in the evening, Atarazana 9 has live music and groups of revellers.

Alcázar de Colón
🔏 185 E4
🕐 Daily 9–5
💷 Inexpensive

Museo de las Atarazanas
🔏 185 E4
🕐 Daily 9–5
💷 Inexpensive

PLAZA ESPAÑA: INSIDE INFO

Top tip Plaza España has a very **different atmosphere** in the day, when it is reasonably quiet; and the evening, when groups of friends unwind with a few drinks and music.

Hidden gem With its fascinating collection of salvaged treasure from sunken galleons the Museo de las Atarazanas receives relatively few visitors. It's an excellent place to learn more of the DR's history.

❹ Calle El Conde

This street bisects the Zona Colonial, running east from the Puerta del Conde (Gate of the Count) to the Río Ozama (River Ozama) about 1km (0.6 miles) away. It was once the town's main road for traffic but was closed in the 1970s and is now a pedestrian precinct full of tempting window displays where you can wander freely and shop to your heart's content.

The Puerta del Conde is named after the Count of Peñalba, who successfully defended the city against a British attack in 1655. It is proudly regarded by Dominicans as the spot where the first Dominican flag was raised in 1844 when independence was declared.

The small park behind it is called Parque Independencia, which also contains the Altar de la Patria, a mausoleum to the country's three greatest heroes – Duarte, Mella and Sanchez.

Along Calle El Conde you can find a few interesting old buildings, but the main interest here is shopping. The street is a varied mix of jewellery shops, fast food outlets, souvenir shops, music stores and fashion boutiques. If you want to take home a taste of *merengue* or *bachata* music, try Musicalia at number 464 for tapes and CDs.

Bustling crowds enjoy an afternoon of shopping along Calle El Conde

TAKING A BREAK

For a taste of *Cocina Dominicana*, **Aljibe Café** (➤ 61) has a bustling atmosphere with good local dishes, just round the corner on Calle Hostos.

➕ 185 D4 ✉ Between the Río Ozama and Puerta del Conde

CALLE EL CONDE: INSIDE INFO

Top tip Think twice before buying cheap CDs. Apart from being illegal, such **pirated discs** are often flawed and frustrating to listen to.

5 Malecón

Its official name is Avenida George Washington, but all locals know it simply as "El Malecón" – the city's seafront promenade. Closed to traffic on Sundays, the broad boulevard is a favourite spot for joggers in the morning and evening, and for diners and dancers at night.

El Obelisco with its anti-Trujillo murals

The Malecón runs west from Fortaleza San José, where a huge statue of Fray Montesino commemorates this brave priest who spoke out against the genocide of the Taínos during the 16th century. Further west along the street are two towering concrete monuments known as La Obelisca and El Obelisco. They were both erected during the Trujillo era (➤ 10), though El Obelisco nowadays bears murals dedicated to the three Mirabal sisters assassinated under Trujillo's orders.

With views overlooking the Caribbean, it is not surprising that many of the city's major hotels have chosen this location, along with shopping malls and hundreds of bars and restaurants. The Malecón really comes to life after dark, when city dwellers come here to eat, drink or just take a stroll and watch the crowds passing by. There are countless places to stop and enjoy a good meal or drink, and most establishments keep the *merengue* playing as if there were no tomorrow. The Malecón is at its best during the annual Merengue Festival in July (➤ 12).

TAKING A BREAK
D'Luis Parillada (➤ 61) is an Argentine-style grill station that gets very popular late at night.

➕ 184 C3 ✉ Avenida George Washington

MALECÓN: INSIDE INFO

Top tip Despite bordering the Caribbean, there is no beach and the waters are not only polluted but also occasionally **shark-infested**, so don't even think of swimming here.

At Your Leisure

⑥ Museo de Ámbar

Dominican amber (► 26) is widely reputed to be the best in the world, and you may be tempted to buy a piece of this beautiful substance during your stay. There are several shops selling amber made into various types of jewellery, and some of them, like the Museo de Ámbar (Amber Museum) conveniently located on the north side of Parque Colón, attract would-be buyers with a small museum. You can learn how amber was formed from the sap of a particular tree, and why many pieces contain "inclusions" – small insects or leaves frozen in time. After looking at the display upstairs, you can browse the items on sale in the gift shop downstairs.

🔢 185 D4 ✉ El Conde 107
🕐 Mon–Sat 9–5 💰 Inexpensive

⑦ Museo de Larimar

Larimar is a beautiful stone of sky-blue colour that can be found only in the Dominican Republic, so it makes for a perfect reminder of your stay here. The Museo de Larimar (Larimar Museum) is situated just around the corner from the cathedral, and a visit to its upstairs, air-conditioned museum to find out how the stone is formed, mined and

A demonstration of jewellery production at the Museo de Ámbar

worked into jewellery is highly recommended. The exhibits include some marvellous sculptures made from larimar and an interesting consideration of the properties ascribed to the stone (for example, its colour is claimed to have a calming influence on all who look at it). Gorgeous pendants, necklaces and bracelets featuring larimar are on sale downstairs in the gift shop,

🔢 185 E4 ✉ Isabel la Católica 54
🕐 Mon–Sat 8–6, Sun 9–1 💰 Free

Altar de la Patria, one of the attractions in Parque Independencia

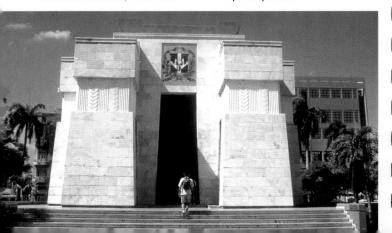

Columbus – The Eternal Traveller

Though visitors to the Dominican Republic are told that Christopher Columbus's remains were once interred in the Catedral de Santa María la Menor, and are now in the huge mausoleum at Faro a Colón, the truth is far from certain. It is generally believed that he was buried in Spain after his death in 1506, and a tomb in Seville attests that his remains are still there. However, his relics were shipped backwards and forwards between Spain and other countries several times, and Cuba and Italy also claim that the "Great Navigator" now rests in their land. It seems that, in death as in life, Columbus's restless spirit will not stay still. Yet his constant roaming may be about to end, as plans are afoot to use DNA testing to determine which of the claimants is correct.

8 Mercado Modelo

Located just north of the Zona Colonial on Avenida Mella, the Mercado Modelo is the place to go shopping for souvenirs. The covered market is split into several narrow alleys, each of which contains a cluster of small shops stacked to the rafters with an incredible range of products. Apart from the usual gift items like amber, larimar, coral, local and Haitian paintings, cigars and musical instruments, there are also carnival masks, batiks, ceramics, candles, T-shirts, CDs and religious paraphernalia. The crowded passageways are a pickpocket's dream, so keep a tight hold of your wallet and when you want to make a purchase, start bargaining in a firm but friendly manner. All displayed prices can be reduced by between 10 per cent and

A model of Columbus' ship, Faro a Colón

50 per cent, and if you buy more than one item from the same stall, discounts can be even greater.

If you turn right (west) on leaving the Mercado Modelo and walk a few steps, you will catch the alluring aroma of freshly-ground coffee. A few steps later you will see an open-fronted shop where the local blend is on sale at an unbelievably cheap price per kilo.

🔁 185 D4 ✉ Avenida Mella
🕓 Mon–Sat 9–12:30, 2:30–5

9 Parque Independencia

Located to the west of Puerta del Conde, just outside the old city walls, this park provides a perfect spot to take a rest between explorations of the many attractions in the

Zona Colonial. Though the roads surrounding it are always busy, the park itself has a restful feel, with several benches in the shade of trees. The park also contains a huge mausoleum called Altar de la Patria, built in 1976. A stony-faced military guard is on constant duty, prohibiting entry to any visitors who are not dressed respectfully, and inside are marble statues of the country's founding fathers – Duarte, Mella and Sanchez.

🔢 185 C4 ✉ West of Puerta del Conde, which is on Palo Hincado

🔟 Hospital de San Nicolás de Bari

The Dominican Republic's string of "firsts" seems endless – first cathedral in the Americas, first street in the Americas, and here, tucked away on Calle Hostos is the first hospital in the Americas. Unlike many other monuments in the Zona Colonial, this one is in ruins, but as such has a feeling of great age. It was built in 1503 under the instructions of Nicolás de Ovando to provide relief for the city's poor. It stood throughout foreign invasions, hurricanes and earthquakes until 1911, when much of it was pulled down as it had become unsafe and was considered a threat to passers-by. You can just about make out the image of a cross on the ground which formed the base of the hospital, and the Renaissance pillars and Gothic arches still create an aura of grandeur, though its only inhabitants these days are thousands of pigeons.

🔢 185 D4 ✉ Calle Hostos, near Las Mercedes 👆 Free

⓫ Convento de los Dominicos

Situated further south on Calle Hostos is the site of the first ever university in the Americas. A convent was founded here in 1510, and when Pope Paul III visited in 1538, he was sufficiently impressed by the lectures in theology he heard that he bestowed upon it the title of "university". The university has long since been moved to another location, but this ancient building, with decorative pillars and elaborate carvings on the facade and striking images of religious figures on the ceiling of the Chapel of the Rosary inside, still holds daily services each morning and evening.

🔢 185 D4 ✉ Calle Hostos at Calle Padre Billini 🕐 Irregular hours 👆 Free

The first hospital in the Americas, Hospital de San Nicolás de Bari

12 Museo de Arte Moderno

Though there are several small museums in the Zona Colonial, the city's major museums are all located around the Plaza de la Cultura in Gazcue, west of the Zona Colonial. Of these perhaps the most interesting is the Museo de Arte Moderno (Museum of Modern Art), which has temporary exhibitions on the first and fourth floors, and permanent exhibitions on the second and third floors. Dominican art is characterised by bold colours. Its major proponents, like Candido Bido, whose work is displayed on the second floor, produce thought-provoking canvases that sometimes idealise island lifestyles and at other times depict everyday scenes as demonic rites.

184 A4 ⊠ **Plaza de la Cultura** 🕐 **Tue–Sun 9–5** 💲 **Inexpensive**

Above: Convento de los Dominicos is the oldest university in the New World

Below: A modern sculpture in the Plaza de la Cultura

🔞 Jardín Botánico

This botanic garden is a must for anyone with a horticultural bent, even though it is located in the suburb of Arroyo Hondo, in the northwest of the city, quite a way from the centre. Over 200 types of palms and over 300 types of orchids are among the plants on display in the extensive gardens. One highlight is the Japanese garden, with its trim shrubs, a pagoda and benches beside a gurgling stream. There are also examples of the mahogany tree, which is the national plant, and pretty water lilies in the aquatic ponds. A shuttle service runs to various parts of the 182ha (450 acres) site, which can be a blessing in the fierce heat of midday.

➕ 182 A2 ✉ Avenida Jardín Botánico and Los Proceres ⏰ Tue–Sun 9–5 💲 Inexpensive

🔞 Faro a Colón

El Faro a Colón (The Lighthouse to Columbus) is one of Santo Domingo's most controversial structures. This concrete monolith, located on the east bank of the Río Ozama, opened in 1992 to commemorate the 500th anniversary of Columbus' first arrival in the Americas. The 800m-long (2,624 feet) building looks nothing like a lighthouse; in fact it is in the shape of a cross that houses a mausoleum holding Columbus' ashes, or so it is claimed (➤ 55), under a 24-hour guard of honour. On the first floor are paintings of the Virgin Mary from all over the Americas, and on the third floor is a small naval museum. The controversy over the building started when hundreds of families were evicted from the area in which it was built. But it didn't end there. The main feature used to be a laser crucifix which was projected onto the sky at night, visible for a wide area around Santo Domingo. The total cost of the project was in excess of $100 million. However, the huge amount of power necessary to light up the lasers caused frequent electricity cuts for towns around the country, so it was switched on less and less often and at present is not being used at all.

➕ 185 F5 ✉ Avenida Mirador del Este ⏰ Daily 10–5 💲 Inexpensive

🔞 Acuario Nacional

If you want to see sharks, stingrays, manatees and other beasts of the deep without having to dive to the bottom of the ocean, visit the Acuario Nacional (National Aquarium). Here you can walk beneath a huge tank, protected by a tunnel of Plexiglas, and watch these sea creatures at play. There is also a pool with endangered turtles. There are no signs in English, and the aquarium is away from the city centre, across the Río Ozama.

➕ 182 B2 ✉ Avenida España ☎ 592 1509 ⏰ Tue–Sun 9–5:30 💲 Inexpensive

Visitors walking through the Plexiglas tunnel in the Acuario Nacional

Where to... Stay

Prices

Expect to pay per double room per night, excluding 22 per cent tax (10 per cent service charge, 12 per cent government tax)

$ under US$50
$$ US$50–100
$$$ over US$100

El Beaterio Guest House $–$$

Set in a quiet street a couple of blocks southeast of Parque Colón in the Zona Colonial, this is a real gem of a colonial building. It has a feeling of considerable age, and with walls almost a metre thick, it is wonderfully cool. Room furnishings are basic but quite adequate, and there is a communal lounge area at the front of the building. Staff are polite and eager to please and the atmosphere is pleasantly homely, but its small size (11 rooms) means it is often full.

★ 185 E4 ☒ Duarte 8 ☎ 687 8657; fax: 687 8657;
Elbeaterio@netscape.net

Conde de Peñalba $$

With arguably the best location of any hotel in the city, this small, colonial-style building overlooks the Parque Colón and Catedral de Santa María la Menor in the heart of the Zona Colonial. The rooms are very comfortably appointed if not particularly spacious, with cable TV and well-equipped bathrooms. Small balconies offer postcard views of the square and cathedral from most rooms, but there are a few rooms without windows at less expensive rates.

★ 185 D4 ☒ Corner of Calle El Conde and Arzobispo Meriño ☎ 688 7121; fax: 688 7535;
www.condepenalba.com

El Embajador $$$

This large hotel is a long-standing favourite of business visitors to the city because of its comprehensive facilities, particularly in the Club Miguel Angel rooms on the top floors. Located just off the Malecón, its top rooms have good views out over the Caribbean, and its gardens are beautifully landscaped, with tennis courts and an attractive swimming pool. The hotel played a small part in the city's history too, playing host to American forces during the 1965 invasion of the island.

★ 182 A2 ☒ Sarasota 65 ☎ 221 2131; fax: 532 5306;
www.occidental-hotels.com

Hostal Hostos $

One of the few decent budget hotel options in the city, with an excellent location just opposite the Monasterio de San Francisco, Hostal Hostos is within easy walking distance of most sights in the Zona Colonial. Guests have free use of a big kitchen, making it possible to prepare your own food and save even more on expenses. One of the suites has a great view across the Zona Colonial, and discounts can be given if you stay for several days.

★ 185 D4 ☒ Calle Hostos 299 ☎ 688 9192; fax: 682 1245

Hostal Nicolas Nader $$

This smart but small place is situated just a couple of short blocks from Parque Colón and Calle El Conde, so is well-placed for both seeing the sights and for shopping. There are only ten rooms here, but all are spacious, with high ceilings and attractive decor, and the building itself is built of limestone with a very colonial character. As well as a restaurant and bar, the small courtyard houses an art gallery.

★ 185 D4 ☒ Luperón 151 on the corner with Duarte ☎ 687 6674; fax: 565 6204; hostal@naders.com

El Napolitano $$

Of all the hotels along the Malecón, the long-established El Napolitano offers the best combination of comfort and economy. Its 70 rooms are compact but clean and well-equipped, with air-conditioning, TVs, smartly fitted bathrooms and good sea views. It also has a popular casino and nightclub, as well as a terrace bar and restaurant beside its small pool. The hotel is only a short walk from the Zona Colonial, but probably its most attractive feature is the competitive rates, which are far less expensive than other hotels along this strip.

🚪 184 C3 ✉ Avenida George Washington 101 ☎ 687 1131/39; fax: 687 8814; www.hotelnapolitano.com

Palacio $$

A beautifully restored and very comfortable colonial building well located just north of the Calle El Conde Promenade. Once home to the family of mid-19th century President Buenaventura Báez, the hotel is stylishly furnished and offers comfortable rooms with a mini-fridge, air conditioning and cable TV. There's a good restaurant and shaded, colonnaded

inner courtyard, safe parking and internet access for guests.

🚪 185 D4 ✉ Duarte 106 on the corner with Salome Ureña ☎ 682 4730; fax: 687 5535; hotelpalacio@codetel.net.do

⏺⏺⏺ Renaissance Jaragua $$$

Run by the Marriott hotel chain, this place is a long-standing favourite with overseas Dominicans, so it is something of a local institution. It is probably the pick of the many big hotels on the Malecón, boasting among its amenities four restaurants, a gym, a pool and hot tub, a tropical garden and indoor lagoon. Most of the large rooms have good views and the service is very attentive.

🚪 184 B3 ✉ Avenida George Washington 367 ☎ 221 2222; fax: 686 0582; h.jaragua@codetel.net.do

⏺⏺⏺ Santo Domingo $$$

For its spacious and comfortable rooms, great range of facilities and

impeccable service, this is one of the best places in town, although it is quite far from the centre. The rooms are well equipped with huge double beds, desk and chair, cable TV and mini-bar. Furnishings are plush and the décor attractive. For a slightly higher rate, you can get a room in the Excel Club and be entitled to use the business facilities. Rates include a fantastic breakfast buffet, and other amenities include a good-sized swimming pool, tennis courts and a fitness centre.

🚪 182 A2 ✉ Corner of Avenida Independencia and Avenida Abraham Lincoln ☎ 221 1511; fax: 535 4050; www.hotel.stodgo.com

⏺⏺⏺ Sofitel Francés $$$

This is another small but well-appointed hotel in the Zona Colonial, where the 16th-century building has been recently renovated, and rooms have period furnishings along with cable TV, a safe deposit box and other modern amenities. The hotel's restaurant, Le

Patio, is very elegant but also very expensive, while the courtyard is a peaceful spot to relax.

🚪 185 D4 ✉ Las Mercedes on the corner with Arzobispo Meriño ☎ 685 9331; fax: 685 1289; H2137@accor-hotels.com

⏺⏺⏺ Sofitel Nicolás de Ovando $$$

If you'd like the experience of staying in a tastefully converted colonial building and money is no object, then this new place located in the Calle de las Damas, might be the place for you. The building's pedigree could hardly be more impressive. Originally the home of Nicolás de Ovando, first governor of the Americas, it is listed as a historic building by UNESCO, though there are many modern features and half the rooms are completely new. Rooms have all the amenities and the service is top class.

🚪 185 E4 ✉ Calle de las Damas ☎ 685 9955; fax: 686 6590; www.sofitel.com, www.accorhotels.com

Where to...
Eat and Drink

Prices

Expect to pay per person for a meal, excluding drinks, tips and tax (22 per cent)
$ under US$2   **$$** US$2–5   **$$$** over US$5

Aljibe Café $–$$

This place in the Zona Colonial has a clever double identity: in the day it is a cosy restaurant serving a variety of staples at reasonable prices; while at night it is a popular bar and live music venue, though food is still available from the kitchen. Apart from the main bar area, there are small, intimate alcoves and a patio area out the back. The clientele are not generally tourists but the staff go out of their way to make everyone feel at home. Check it out for a satisfying lunch while exploring the Zona Colonial on foot, or drop by in the evening to listen to local bands and get to know local people.

🚹 185 D4 ⊠ Calle Hostos 156
☎ 687 6327 🕙 Daily 11:30 am–late

La Atarazana $$–$$$

Conveniently situated on the edge of the Plaza España, this former warehouse has been successfully converted into a stylish and appealing restaurant. The historic building has an intimate courtyard and an air-conditioned room upstairs. Tiled floors, wrought-iron window frames and potted plants give the place an air of elegance. The daily buffet is very popular, but there is also a great choice of à la carte dishes, both Dominican and international.

🚹 185 E4 ⊠ Atarazana 5 ☎ 689
2900 🕙 Daily noon–midnight

El Conde $–$$

Though located right on the Parque Colón in the heart of the Zona Colonial, this no-frills café/restaurant serves a range of filling local foods and international dishes at very reasonable prices. It is part of the Conde de Peñalba Hotel which occupies the upper floors. Some of the tables are located inside but the most popular ones are outside in the shade of umbrellas and a pipal tree. This is one of the best people-watching spots in town and it is easy to while away hours over a coffee or a beer watching the constant parade of humanity busily passing by.

🚹 185 D4 ⊠ Parque Colón ☎ 682
6944 🕙 Daily 8 am–midnight

D'Luis Parillada $–$$

If you're feeling hungry late at night, make your way down to the Malecón and fill yourself with grilled meat while shuffling to the incessant merengue beat. The speciality here is Argentine-style grilled meat; huge portions that can be slow in coming but will certainly fill you up when they do. Seating is outdoor with the sound of the ocean crashing on rocks nearby. Prices are extremely low, so it's hardly surprising that the place draws in crowds night after night.

🚹 185 D3 ⊠ Plaza Montesino,
Malecón 🕙 Daily 24 hours

Lina $$$

Thought by many to be the best restaurant in the city, if not the country, the Lina is located in the Gran Hotel Lina in Gazcue district. The place certainly impresses with its elegant ambience, striking floral displays and immaculately dressed waiters. Customers tend to dress accordingly. The menu features

Spanish, Italian and other international cuisines, and the choices are tough. Will it be oysters or smoked salmon? Grouper or red snapper? Veal or chicken? Though prices are not cheap, they are not sky-high, and pasta dishes are particularly good value. Guests are serenaded by a pianist playing romantic songs in the evening.

+ 184 A4 **⊠** Gran Hotel Lina, Avenida Máximo Gómez at the corner of Avenida 27 de Febrero **☎** 563 5000 **◎** Daily noon–4, 6:30–midnight

Museo de Jamón $$–$$$

On the western side of Plaza España is a string of restaurants that are all very popular with tourists and well-to-do locals, particularly in the evenings when musicians often entertain diners. It takes its name from the huge ham shanks hanging from the ceiling in the typical style of an old-fashioned Spanish *tapas* bar. Sample small dishes of tasty snacks such as stuffed olives, Spanish tortilla (omelette) or meatballs in sauce, which can be nibbled as an accompaniment to wine or sherry.

+ 185 E4 **⊠** Atarazana 17 **☎** 688 9644 **◎** Daily 11 am–midnight

Paparazzo $$$

Already established in Santiago, Paparazzo has recently opened its doors in the capital, and the combination of Dominican fusion food and intimate ambience is sure to make it a firm favourite with diplomats, businessmen, lovers and friends. There are a variety of eating areas, and the decorative motifs are brick walls, dark wood furniture and scented candles. There is a private room for a group of 30 people and a "dessert room", where guests can enjoy cakes, coffee and cigars. The menu has some mouth-watering and original dishes, as well as a wonderful version of the national favourite *chivo guisado*, or goat stew. The seafood dishes are fresh and excellent, particularly the lobster. There is also a wide range of

wines and spirits along with domestic and imported beers at the bar.

+ 182 A2 **⊠** Roberto Pastoriza 313 **☎** 540 5000; fax: 540 5007; Paparazzosd@codetel.net.do **◎** Daily noon–late

Pat'e Palo European Brasserie $$–$$$

This is perhaps the most popular bar and restaurant on the west side of Plaza España, its name meaning "Peg Leg" after a famous pirate. The wide-ranging menu includes a great number of fish dishes and some tempting desserts. Prices are a bit on the steep side as this place caters predominantly to tourists but the well-prepared food does not disappoint.

+ 185 E4 **⊠** Atarazana 25 **☎** 687 8089 **◎** Daily 4 pm–1 am

Restaurant Bucanero $$$

A restaurant with fine views across the Río Ozama to the Zona Colonial. It's not the cheapest place in town, but the food is consistently

good and the menu extensive. House specialities include filete de res bucanero or beef fillet in a red wine sauce and mero bucanero, or sea bass stuffed with a delicious mixture of crab, lobster and shrimp. The seafood is really fresh.

+ 185 F3 **⊠** Puerto de Santo Domingo **☎** 592 2202 **◎** 11 am–midnight

Vesuvio $$$

Located down on the Malecón, this is a long-standing favourite for both locals and visitors, serving up excellent Italian fare in a somewhat formal setting. The menu includes a wide range of pasta dishes such as mostaccioli, gnocchi and penne, as well as many fish and beef dishes. Prices reflect the consistently high quality of the food. Next door is a pizzeria, also called Vesuvio and run by the same owners, that is less formal and includes snacks like sandwiches and crêpes.

+ 184 A2 **⊠** Malecón 521 **☎** 221 3333 **◎** noon–midnight

Where to... Shop

Whether it's amber or larimar, cigars or rum, Haitian art or stylish clothes that you're after, you're likely to find what you're looking for in Santo Domingo. The pedestrianised **Calle El Conde** and the maze of alleys in the **Mercado Modelo** are particularly good hunting grounds, while several **modern shopping malls are scattered around the centre.**

For an overview of what is on offer, take a stroll down **Calle El Conde** (▶ 52) and browse the windows as you go. You will see shops selling amber and larimar, Dominican cigars, *merengue* and *bachata* music, books and stylish clothes. Since the street is closed to traffic, you can take your time wandering along here, taking a rest on the benches that are placed conveniently along the street or re-charging the batteries at one of the many fast-food outlets or cafés.

Towards the eastern end, Calle El Conde runs through **Parque Colón**, where you may be tempted to buy yourself a piece of **amber** (▶ 26) at the **Museo de Ámbar** (▶ 54). Amber makes a very unique and distinctive gift, and is worked into pieces of jewellery of all different sizes and prices. The museum has a good range of amber items for sale, but their prices tend to be a bit steep. For less inexpensive items, check out **The Swiss Mine** at 101 El Conde, also facing Parque Colón.

Just round the corner from Parque Colón on Isabel La Católica, the **Museo de Larimar** (▶ 54) has probably the most impressive display of larimar jewellery in the entire country. Once again, prices are on the expensive side, but the workmanship is top class. In many ways, larimar is an even better souvenir to buy than amber, as it is unique to this country.

One of the most enjoyable places to shop for Dominican souvenirs and gifts is the **Mercado Modelo** (▶ 55), located just north of the Zona Colonial on Avenida Melia. Allow a couple of hours to root around the many stalls which sell an unbelievable range of goods, including original paintings and ceramics. On the steps leading up to the market are several stalls selling *mamajuana*, a strange mixture of herbs and bark that is sold in bottles. When mixed with water, the resulting potion forms a kind of tonic that is purported to be good for sexual stamina.

The vibrant colours of **Haitian and Dominican paintings** are on sale all across the country, often creating eye-catching displays. The cheapest, small canvases sell for a couple of dollars, but if you are looking to buy quality work, you need to track down a specialist shop. For Haitian paintings, check out **Galería Elín** at Arzobispo Meriño 203 near Parque Colón or for work by Dominican artists, head for **Galería Bidó** at Calle Dr Baez 5 (Mon–Fri 9–1; tel: 685 5310).

Another souvenir widely associated with Caribbean history and particularly the *real* **Spanish coins**, especially the *real* silver coins known as "pieces of eight". These sell for around US$100 at the Museo de las Atarazanas (▶ 51) and provide an interesting and very tangible link with the historical past of the "Spanish Main" and the era of pirates and buccaneers.

If you feel the need to visit a shopping mall where you can find designer clothes and other familiar items, **Plaza Central** at the corner of 27 de Febrero and Troncoso is centrally located and also houses **a cinema.**

Where to...
Be Entertained

The city's historical sights and shops may have plenty of interest to keep you busy in the daytime but its nightlife is also fantastic. In fact it is so good, there is every chance you will stay up all night and miss the next day's sightseeing. Apart from bars and nightclubs, there's a very wide choice of venues offering live music and dance, particularly in and around the Zona Colonial. There are also plenty of casinos, theatres, cinemas, cultural centres and frequent festivals that present a bewildering but satisfying choice of entertainment activities for all.

BARS AND NIGHTCLUBS

Listening and dancing to *merengue* and *bachata* music is the national pastime in the DR, and an evening spent joining in is an absolute must during any visit to the country. Fortunately there are plenty of venues to choose from, and if you are staying in one of the hotels along the **Malecón**, you may find that you need go no further than your hotel's nightclub. Those in the **Renaissance Jaragua** and **El Napolitano** are particularly popular. A bit further west on Avenida Mirador del Sur, the **Guá Cara Taína** is the place most frequented by tourists. It is a huge, multi-level cave where live bands perform popular international and regionalhits nightly.

The **Zona Colonial** also has more than its fair share of bars where live musicians entertain in the evenings. Those that ring the west side of the Plaza España are a good place to look for action, particularly **Atarazana 9**, but there are plenty of other alternatives. If you're more in the mood to tune in to the local vibe, try somewhere like the **Aljibe Café** (▶ 61).

CASINOS

If you love a flutter, you'll find no shortage of other punters in the many casinos that announce their presence with extravagant neon signs. The **Hispaniola Hotel**, right next to the Santo Domingo Hotel (▶ 60) has probably the most extravagant sign in town and countless ways to risk your cash.

THEATRES AND CINEMAS

If it's high culture you're after, search the local press, such as the Spanish language newspaper, *Listín Diario*, for information about **opera, ballet and symphony** performances at the Teatro Nacional or the Palacio de Bellas Artes.

If a Hollywood blockbuster is more to your taste, call one of the cinemas in the shopping malls to check if the soundtrack is in English or Spanish.

FESTIVALS

There is a festival taking place almost every month in the Dominican Republic (▶ 11), and a couple of them are such fun that they are even worth planning your holiday around. On each Sunday in February, Carnival is celebrated on Calle El Conde and the Malecón, while from late July to early August, the Malecón hosts the annual **Merengue Festival**, the DR's most vibrant and colourful happening. These events provide a golden opportunity to have fun and make friends with the local people.

North Coast

Getting Your Bearings

The north coast of the Dominican Republic is one of the most popular regions of the country, and it is easy to see why. Not only does it have a seemingly endless string of beautiful beaches, but also the historic town of Puerto Plata and the site of Columbus's first settlement in the DR at La Isabela.

Los Siete Hermanos

Monte Cristi

5

Gran Mangle

Jaiquí ○
La Cañada

El
Manantial ○
El
Charcazo

Los
Conúcos ○

Higuerito ○

**Cayo
Paraíso** **6**

**Parque Nacional
La Isabela**

Bahía Isabela **7**

Punta Rucia
Estero Hondo ○

○ La Rusia

○ Luperón

45

20

30

30

29

The great majority of visitors stay in the huge all-inclusive resorts just east of Puerto Plata at Playa Dorada, where there are no less than 14 hotels along the beach. These resorts provide everything a holidaymaker could want, but it would be a shame to be in the area without taking a look at the quaint Victorian-style houses, the amber museum and Fortaleza de San Felipe (Fort San Felipe) in Puerto Plata. Another experience not to be missed is a ride on the cable car up to the peak of Isabel de Torres to get a sweeping view over the town and coast.

Further afield, the islands to the west off the coast of Monte Cristi, Punta Rucia and La Isabela are a wonderland for snorkellers, while to the east the towns of Sosúa and Cabarete are very popular among independent travellers. Both have excellent beaches, and Cabarete is a kaleidoscope of colour with windsurfers and kitesurfers riding the waves. Even further east, the quiet town of Río San Juan has a tranquil lagoon, Laguna Gri Gri, and nearby Playa Grande is one of the most popular beaches on the coast.

**Previous page:
Windsurfing at Cabarete
Below: Sipping fresh
coconuts, Playa Dorada**

Cable car to Pico Isabel de Torres

1 **2** Puerto Plata

Monte Llano

o Caliche

3 Sosúa

4 Cabarete

Bahía Escondida

Río San Juan and Laguna Gri Gri **8**

Playa Grande **9**

0   20 km

0   10 miles

o El Tablón

o Río Piedra

Gaze down on the Atlantic coastline from Pico Isabel de Torres, explore the historic buildings in downtown Puerto Plata, and check out the beach haunts of Sosúa and Cabarete.

North Coast in Three Days

Day One

Morning

Head for the entrance to the **❶ cable car** (➤ 70) to the southwest of Puerto Plata, for the ride to the top of **Pico Isabel de Torres**. Enjoy the spectacular views at the summit and descend at your leisure past brightly painted houses (above).

Afternoon

After the stimulating altitude of the mountain, you should have a healthy appetite. Head back into town and sit down for lunch at one of the many restaurants near **Parque Central** (also known as Parque Independencia), then begin an exploration of **❷ Puerto Plata** (➤ 71) with its delightful Victorian houses. Also check out the 16th century fortress, **Fortaleza de San Felipe** on the coast just north of town.

Evening

Enjoy a leisurely seafood meal at Polanco (➤ 80), then dance to the sounds of *merengue* and *bachata* until the early hours at La Barrica nightclub (➤ 82), which attracts a crowd of locals every night.

Day Two

Morning/Afternoon

If you are curious about historical sites, join a tour to **7 Parque Nacional La Isabela** (➤ 77) to see the remains of Columbus's first settlement in the Dominican Republic. If you would rather look at some of the region's fascinating marine life, take a tour to **6 Cayo Paraíso** (➤ 76) and float around the reefs which are teeming with tropical fish.

Evening

If you are not one for resting, go to Playa Dorada Plaza a few kilometres east of Puerto Plata to check out the nightlife at Hemingway's Café (➤ 82).

Day Three

Morning

Head east along the coast to **3 Sosúa** (➤ 73), historic home to the DR's Jewish community, and check out the chic shops (above) and lovely beach (below).

Afternoon/Evening

Move on east to **4 Cabarete** (➤ 74) a wind and kitesurfer's paradise and one of the country's most popular hangouts for independent travellers. If you don't have to head back or onward in the evening, linger in one of Cabarete's many seafront restaurants.

Cable Car to Pico Isabel de Torres

This outing to look at sweeping views of the Atlantic coast from the top of Pico Isabel de Torres is a memorable experience, especially on a clear day when you can see a good stretch of the Atlantic coast spread out below.

The cable cars hold about 20 people each, but the ride is so popular that you should count on an hour's wait to get up, then the same again to come down. The ten-minute ascent in the cable car and the exhilarating air at over 800m (2,624 feet) snap the senses awake.

From the top, when clear, it is easy to pick out downtown Puerto Plata and **Fortaleza de San Felipe** (➤ 72) jutting out into the Atlantic. To the east (right) of town stands the vast bottling factory of Brugal Rum, and beyond that lie the all-inclu-sives at Playa Dorada. Crowning the summit is a 16m (52 feet) replica of the enormous Corcovado statue of Jesus in Río de Janeiro. A popular souvenir photo is to pose two friends beneath the outstretched arms of Christ, so it looks as if He is touching their heads in blessing.

On the way up Pico Isabel de Torres

TAKING A BREAK

There is a café selling drinks and snacks at the base of the cable car ride, and a refreshment kiosk at the top.

➕ 181 E5
✉ Entrance is on Avenida Teleférico, southwest of Puerto Plata, off Avenida

Circunvalación Sur
☎ 586 2122
🕐 Daily 8:30–5
💲 Moderate

PICO ISABEL DE TORRES: INSIDE INFO

Top tips Though this is a great trip on a clear day, it is hardly worth it when overcast. Plan to go up in the morning as the peak often clouds over at midday.

• To **avoid a queue**, turn up at around 8 am.

• Don't forget to take along your **camera** and binoculars if you have them.

2 Puerto Plata

Puerto Plata is the largest town on the north coast of the DR, and is well worth a visit to see its quaint Victorian houses, its amber museum and its 16th century fort. The town also hosts frequent festivals and has a vibrant nightlife.

Puerto Plata (Silver Port) was given its name by Columbus on his historic 1492 voyage. Some think that it was named for the sunlight sparkling on the water in the bay, while others believe it was from the silver-coloured backs of leaves in the wind. Despite its honourable origins, the town was often skirted by sailing vessels in the 16th and 17th century due to its reputation for **piracy**. In fact it was not until the late 19th century that it prospered as one of the main centres in the **tobacco** boom. It was during this era that the picturesque "gingerbread" houses were built, the main features of which are elaborately carved balconies, friezes and window frames.

A good place to begin an exploration of the town is **Parque Central**, right in the centre. All the buildings surrounding the square are attractive and worth a close look, particularly the **Catedral San Felipe**, with its art deco design. There are several shops in the vicinity that stock a wide range of typical Dominican souvenirs. The neighbouring streets are lined with some delightful examples of Victorian architecture.

One beautifully preserved example of this architecture is the **Museo de Ámbar**, where the upstairs museum presents the fascinating process by which amber is formed, with clear explanations in English. There are several examples of "inclusions" – insects, leaves or lizards in an eternal embrace

Fortaleza de San Felipe is the oldest structure in Puerto Plata

within the translucent substance. The back lighting shows off this fossilised resin in all its glory, and the temptation to buy a souvenir in the shop downstairs is strong indeed.

On a spur of land to the north of the old city, **Fortaleza de San Felipe** juts out into the Atlantic. Though it was built to protect the city and the bay, it has more often been put to use as a prison, holding dignitaries such as Juan Pablo Duarte, one of the nation's founding fathers. The fort was the only building in the city to survive a blaze in 1605, making it the oldest structure in town. You can clamber around the towers and gun turrets, or nose into the old prison, where there is a small museum with a few prisoners' shackles and cannonballs on display.

TAKING A BREAK

There is a small snack bar in the grounds of the Museo de Ámbar, but if you are looking for something more substantial, head for **Sam's Bar** (▶ 80) near Parque Central, which offers Western dishes such as burgers and steaks, as well as daily specials.

Parque Central is also referred to as Parque Independencia

Museo de Ámbar
✚ 186 C2
✉ Calle Duarte, east of Parque Central
☎ 320 8714; www.ambermuseum.com
🕐 Mon–Sat 9–6
💰 Inexpensive

Fortaleza de San Felipe
✚ 186 B1
✉ Avenida General Gregorio Luperón
🕐 Thu–Tue 9–noon, 2–5
💰 Inexpensive

PUERTO PLATA: INSIDE INFO

Top tip In Parque Central or at Fortaleza de San Felipe, you are likely to be approached by **freelance guides** offering to show you around, though their services are not really necessary. Be firm in your refusal, or you may find them tagging around after you.

In more detail To find out more information about what's going on in and around town, log on to www.popreport.com
• To find out about events such as **concerts or exhibitions** in town, check out www.puertoplatainfo.com

3 Sosúa

Located about 25km (15 miles) east of Puerto Plata, Sosúa is a small coastal town with a gorgeous horseshoe-shaped beach of golden sand. Its calm waters are protected by a coral reef, making it ideal for swimming, and its streets are crowded with cosy cafés and handicraft shops.

Sosúa's origins lie far from tourism, however. The town was founded in the late 19th century by United Fruit Company as a port from which to ship **bananas** from nearby plantations. Within a couple of decades the business had declined and the town was abandoned until 1940, when in an apparent humanitarian gesture, President Trujillo invited about 350 families of German and Austrian Jews to settle here. Few Jewish residents remain in Sosúa now, but there is still a small **synagogue**. This is located in El Batey.

TAKING A BREAK

Check out **On the Waterfront** at the end of Calle Dr Rosen. It combines stunning views with delicious seafood at moderate prices.

➕ 181 E5

Museo de Sosúa
✉ Calle Martínez
🕐 Mon–Fri 9–1, 2–4
💰 Moderate

By the beach at Sosúa

SOSÚA: INSIDE INFO

Top tip Sosúa's annual **jazz festival** in October attracts top performers from the USA and all over the Caribbean.

In more detail If you want to learn more about the Jewish community in Sosúa visit the **Museo de Sosúa**, next door to the synagogue. It shows the development of the community through photos and personal memorabilia.

❹ Cabarete

Surfing aficionados from all over the world head for Cabarete to try out their skills with sails or, increasingly, with kites. For beginners, several companies offer lessons in either windsurfing or kitesurfing (sometimes also called "kiteboarding") and provide equipment as part of the deal.

Cabarete's history is even shorter than Sosúa's. There was nothing here at all until the 1980s, when the well-known windsurfer, Jean Laporte declared it an ideal beach for the sport. Now it is one of the north coast's most popular destinations, particularly for independent travellers, with a glut of cheap hotels, bars, restaurants and convenience stores scattered along the main road.

Being relatively new, the town is somewhat characterless, though the partying antics of the surfing crowd means that the town buzzes till late and the beach is often deserted in the morning. Also, afternoons are usually better for a good breeze, which is why it is wiser to visit then.

The bay itself seems designed for **windsurfing**, with prevailing winds from the east making it easy for surfers to get out to the reef and then ride the waves back in to the humorously named **Bozo Beach**. Some of the experts perform incredible antics, and it's worth using a pair of binoculars to watch them performing somersaults over the whitecaps.

A couple of kilometres west of Cabarete, on another idyllic white sand beach, exponents of the relatively new sport of **kitesurfing** make for even brighter and more exciting sights than the windsurfers. Using a colourful kite to provide the power instead of a sail, the riders who have mastered the technicalities carry out some daring jumps that windsurfers could not even dream of. On a busy day, the spectacle of bright kites against a blue sky and riders zipping along the waves can be mesmerising.

**Above:
Windsurfers at
Cabarete
Right:
Kitesurfing
near Cabarete**

After dark, Cabarete becomes one of the liveliest places in the country, with very danceable live and recorded music in many **bars** along the central strip.

TAKING A BREAK

Conveniently situated on the central beach, with a good view of all the action, **Casa del Pescador** (➤ 80) serves up great seafood, accompanied with several side dishes, and a strong rum aperitif on the house.

🕂 181 F5
✉ 30km (18 miles) east of Puerto Plata
🚐 *Guagua* from Puerto Plata and Sosuá

A Colourful Coastline

The entire north coast between Monte Cristi and Río San Juan is often referred to as "The Amber Coast" due to the proximity of amber mines to Puerto Plata, yet it is also frequently called "The Silver Coast" after the town of Puerto Plata itself. Another ambiguity concerns the term *Costa del Coco*, or Coconut Coast, which sometimes refers to the east coast around Bávaro and Punta Cana, and at other times to sections of the north coast. (To avoid confusion, this book refers only to north and east coasts.)

CABARETE: INSIDE INFO

Top tips Like Sosúa, Cabarete plays host to a **jazz festival** each October. There is also a month of festivities called Cabarete Alegría in February and an international windsurfing race week in June. At these times, expect to find hotels full and prices high for any available rooms.

• Hotels along the west end of the beach that cater to kitesurfers frequently display ads offering used **equipment for sale**.

At Your Leisure

5 Monte Cristi

Situated in the extreme northwest of the Dominican Republic, Monte Cristi is about as far away from it all as you can get. West of Puerto Plata, the landscape gets progressively more arid as it approaches the Haitian border, but the tiny town of Monte Cristi may be of interest to adventurous types. The main attractions for visitors are the local beaches, particularly Playa Bolanos, and the Parque Nacional Monte Cristi. The eastern part of the park contains El Morro, a towering plateau with steps leading up to the summit. The western part consists of mangroves, lagoons and a cluster of tiny islands called Los Siete Hermanos (The Seven Brothers), where sea turtles lay their eggs. Local hotels can arrange boat trips around the park, where you will likely spot egrets, pelicans and herons.

➕ 180 B5

Parque Nacional Monte Cristi
🕐 Daily 8–5 💲 Inexpensive

Monte Cristi was originally founded in 1533

6 Cayo Paraíso

Cayo Paraíso (Paradise Key) has some of the best snorkelling to be found anywhere in the Caribbean, and trips there can be organised through most hotels on the north coast. A coral reef runs round the island, and the sizes, shapes and colours of the tropical fish that flit in and out of the nooks and crannies is simply astonishing. By contrast, the island itself is nothing more than a strip of sand in the water. The island is reached by speedboat from the mainland port of Punta Rucia, a couple of hours' drive west of Puerto Plata. A few basic huts made of coconut leaves offer a little shade, but most day-trippers prefer to spend their time marvelling over the magical reefs or sunbathing on the soft sand. On the way back, the speedboats pass through narrow mangrove canals, and visitors are then given a late buffet lunch at Punta Rucia before returning to base. Among the most reliable local tour companies, you could try El Paraíso Tours, Puerto Plata (tel: 320 7606, www.cayoparaiso.com)

➕ 180 C5 ✉ Punta Rucia

🮃Parque Nacional La Isabela

Returning to find his first settlement in modern-day Haiti razed to the ground, Columbus sailed further east and founded La Isabela, which he named in honour of the Queen of Spain. Though the location offered a protected bay, there was no fresh water or fertile soil, which soon led to its abandonment in favour of Santo Domingo. Little remains of this settlement today but a museum displays tools, jewellery and coins from the era. The museum also features accounts of the lifestyle of the local Taínos and the colonising Spaniards, as well as a reconstruction of a Taíno settlement outside.

➕ 180 C5 ✉ 50km (31 miles) west of Puerto Plata 🕐 Daily 9–5:30
🎟 Inexpensive

A child plays by the sea in the quiet Dominican town of Río San Juan

🮃Río San Juan and Laguna Gri Gri

If you'd like to wander the streets of a typically Dominican town which is not over-run with foreigners, then Río San Juan is your place. Situated about 65km (40 miles) southeast of Sosúa, Río San Juan has a welcoming feel. It also has a few passable hotels and several restaurants. There are also diving operations working out of here, and popular tours of Laguna Gri Gri, a mangrove lagoon teeming with birds.

➕ 182 A5 ✉ Highway 5, near Parque Nacional Francisco Viejo

🮃Playa Grande

Just a few kilometres east of Río San Juan, Playa Grande is one of the most spectacular strips of sand along the north coast. It is very popular among Dominicans and you can find basic food and drinks at the eastern end. The surf here is strong and the colour of the water is irresistible; but beware of vicious riptides to which lives are lost every year.

➕ 182 A5 ✉ Highway 5, near Parque Nacional Francisco Viejo

Where to... Stay

Prices

Expect to pay per double room per night, excluding 22 per cent tax (10 per cent service charge, 12 per cent government tax)
$ under US$50 $$ US$50–100 $$$ over US$100

CABARETE

Kite Beach Hotel $–$$

Located a few kilometres west of the centre of Cabarete on Kite Beach – the most popular beach for kitesurfers – this hotel is ideal for anyone who wants to learn or practise this new sport. They have a special space to clean and store equipment, which is a necessity with kitesurfing gear. The hotel has 30 rooms (some air-conditioned, some with fans) and 8 air-conditioned suites. A beachfront bar serves a buffet breakfast inclusive in the price, and has a great view of all the action. There is a kitesurfing school on site, and a notice board displaying information of equipment for sale.

✚ 181 F5 ☒ Carretera Punta Goleta, Cabarete ☎ 508 3674; fax: 571 0278; www.kitebeachhotel.com

Villa Taína $$

Located at the west end of Cabarete, this smart place offers top-class accommodation at very competitive prices. The hotel was constructed according to the principles of Feng Shui or Chinese geomancy, a technique of harnessing the positive energy of the environment. It is named after the peace-loving Taíno Indians and is decorated with Taíno artefacts. It has just over 50 rooms of varying size as well as its own pool, and all rooms have air-conditioning as well as a terrace or balcony and cable TV. Several rooms have sea views. In-room internet connections are also available for a supplementary fee. Rates include a breakfast buffet and there is a windsurfing centre at the hotel too.

✚ 181 F5 ☒ Cabarete ☎ 571 0722; fax: 571 0883

PUERTO PLATA

Castilla $

This small place with just nine rooms in the heart of Puerto Plata has simple, clean, unfussy accommodation at rock-bottom prices. In fact Hotel Castilla may well offer the least expensive rooms in the entire country. The Victorian-style building was constructed in the 1890s and claims to have the town's oldest inn on the ground floor, a restaurant and bar that is now called Sam's Bar (➤ 80) The building is painted in bright colours and has picturesque balconies overlooking the street. Some rooms have private bathrooms, and there is also an apartment with kitchen and bathroom to rent by the month.

✚ 181 E5 ☒ Calle José del Carmen Ariza 34, Puerto Plata ☎ 586 7267

Gran Ventana $$$

This is one of the best deals among the all-inclusives at Playa Dorada – spacious, well-equipped rooms, landscaped gardens and a full programme of activities including sports, dancing and games. Guests can eat once a week at the two à la carte restaurants or whenever they like at the buffet, and there's a different show every night at around 9 pm. It's also conveniently situated right next to Playa Dorada Plaza, a maze of boutiques, tour agents and restaurants.

✚ 181 E5 ☒ Playa Dorada, Puerto Plata ☎ 320 2111; fax: 320 4017; granventana@victoriahoteles.com.do

Porto Fino Guest House $

Located about a kilometre east of downtown Puerto Plata in a quiet area near the beach, this single-storey building with only 13 rooms is ideal for those who find resorts with hundreds of rooms overwhelming. The air-conditioned rooms are clean and comfortable, and each has a private hot-water bathroom. There is also a swimming pool set under a sprawling, shady mango tree and a restaurant that serves up tasty, inexpensive *criollo* food.

➕ 181 E5 ☒ Avenida Las Hermanas Mirabal 12, Puerto Plata ☎ 586 2858; fax: 586 5050

Puerto Plata Village $$$

This is a large, all-inclusive resort with a mixture of standard and superior rooms as well as suites, all designed in Victorian style and painted in pastel shades. The site is supposedly based on the streets of Puerto Plata, hence its name, and it is located right next to the golf

course which is free for guests. There are also four restaurants (including a good pizzeria on the beach), four bars, two pools, tennis and volleyball courts. The resort also offers free watersports, though the beach is a bit of a walk. There are no special activities for kids here, so it is better suited to couples or groups looking for a quiet retreat.

➕ 181 E5 ☒ Playa Dorada, Puerto Plata ☎ 320 4012; fax: 320 5113; www.ppvillage.com

Sun Village Beach Resort $$$

Located at Cofresi Beach, a few kilometres west of Puerto Plata and a long way from the concentration of other all-inclusives at Playa Dorada, this resort boasts an impressive array of accommodation and amenities. The standard and deluxe rooms, suites and villas (which sleep up to 10 people!) all have views of the ocean, pool or tropical garden and have furnished outdoor terraces too. Apart from

the buffet, there are no less than five à la carte restaurants. Of the six swimming pools, one is three-tiered and two have swim-up bars, while activities include tennis, horse riding and non-motorised watersports, as well as a special programme for kids.

➕ 181 E5 ☒ Cofresi, near Puerto Plata ☎ 370 3364; www.sunvillagebeachresort.com

SOSÚA

Sosúa Bay Hotel $$$

This beautiful new all-inclusive hotel enjoys an idyllic location on a cliff at the eastern end of Bahía de Sosúa, with a classic view of turquoise waters, golden sands and boats bobbing in the bay. Most of the 193 rooms share this dream-like view, and the colonial design of the building and the attention to detail in decoration enhances the feeling of elegance. There are four restaurants to choose from, three pools, a Jacuzzi and free watersports.

➕ 181 E5 ☒ Calle Dr Alejo Martínez 1, Sosúa ☎ 586 7267; www.starzresorts.com

Waterfront $$

The Waterfront's simple but comfortable rooms are a great deal. With a motto of "no line-ups, no wrist bands, no group games", the hotel is taking a dig at the all-inclusive experience and appealing to individuals who like to take charge of their own entertainment. Likewise, though they have an all-inclusive meal plan, they encourage visitors to get out and sample some of the other hundred or so restaurants in town, though it has to be said that their own is one of the best (➤ 80). The hotel is located to the east of town above a small beach at a place known locally as "look out point". It offers fantastic sunset views from the poolside terrace.

➕ 181 E5 ☒ Calle Dr Rosen 1, Sosúa. ☎ 571 2670; fax: 571 3586; www.hotelwaterfront.com

Where to...
Eat and Drink

Prices

Expect to pay per person for a meal, excluding drinks, tips and tax (22 per cent)
$ under US$2   **$$** US$2–5   **$$$** over US$5

CABARETE

Casa del Pescador $$–$$$

This small eatery right on the beach in the middle of Cabarete does not look particularly special, but it has earned itself a reputation for serving up the best seafood in town against considerable competition. Guests are offered a free rum aperitif on arrival – a clever tactic since everything tastes good after that, whether it be king crab, lobster or seafood spaghetti. All main dishes are served with small side dishes of rice, French fries and salad, and there is a small range of desserts.

🏳 181 F5 ☒ Carretera 5, Cabarete ☎ 571 0760; fax: 571 0804 🕐 Daily 4–11

PUERTO PLATA

Café Cito $$

Run by an expat Canadian, this place describes itself as a "jazz/blues bistro" and specialises in dishes such as fillet mignon, pork chops and chicken breast at moderate prices served to a background of cool sounds. The restaurant recently moved from its location in downtown Puerto Plata to a spot just near the gate to the Playa Dorada all-inclusives, clearly trying to tempt a few visitors to give their buffet a miss for a day. They also organise a weekly pub crawl (▶ 82).

🏳 181 E5 ☒ Plaza Isabela, Km 3.5 Puerto Plata–Sosúa Highway ☎ 586 7923 🕐 Mon–Sat (daily from Christmas to Easter), noon–midnight

Polanco $$

This restaurant occupies a quaint Victorian house in the heart of Puerto Plata, with a shady balcony running around the outside. It serves up some of the best seafood and typical Dominican food in town at very reasonable prices.

🏳 186 C2 ☒ Calle Beller 60, Puerto Plata ☎ 586 9174 🕐 Daily 7.30 am–11.30 pm

Sam's Bar $–$$

This place on the ground floor of Hotel Castilla (▶ 78) in the centre of Puerto Plata caters almost exclusively to foreigners pining for comfort food, and is therefore very popular for breakfast and standard Western dishes such as hamburgers. The daily specials are usually good value, as is the American Breakfast. Prices are inexpensive and there's always a friendly atmosphere.

🏳 186 D2 ☒ Calle José del Carmen Ariza 37, Puerto Plata ☎ 586 7267 🕐 Daily 7 am–midnight

SOSÚA

On The Waterfront $$–$$$

Even if you're not staying at the Waterfront Hotel in Sosúa (▶ 79), it's worth going out of your way to enjoy the fantastic views from this attractive location, particularly at sunset. The speciality here is seafood, and there are plenty of tempting choices, including a great "surf and turf" combination of steak and scampi.

🏳 181 E5 ☒ Calle Dr Rosen 1, Sosúa ☎ 571 2670; fax: 571 3586 🕐 Daily 7 am–11 pm. Happy hour 4–6

Where to...
Shop

What with gift shops in most hotels, hawkers scouring the beach for customers, and attractive boutiques lining the streets, shopping is never a problem on the north coast of the Dominican Republic. The resort town of Puerto Plata offers the widest choice of wares, but there are also some good shopping opportunities at Playa Dorado

Though some souvenirs are on sale in the hotels and resorts of the region – particularly the all-inclusives – the range of items is limited. However, it is possible to combine a sight-seeing tour of **Puerto Plata** with some serious shopping in the well-stocked hand-

icraft and gift shops near **Parque Central**. The **Canoa** (Calle Beller, open daily 9–6) has some very appealing figures carved from mango and mahogany wood, and an impressive selection of **jewellery** designed from amber, larimar and black coral, although it should be noted that black coral is an endangered species. Behind the shop is a workshop, where you might chance upon a painter or carver at work. Another good hunting ground for gifts is the **Galería de Ámbar** (Calle 12 de Julio, open Mon–Sat 8:30–6), not to be confused with the **Museo de Ámbar** (▶ 54), which also has a good gift shop. Upstairs is a small museum displaying Dominican handicrafts and products, while downstairs is a comprehensive range of gift products like T-shirts, Haitian paintings and amber jewellery.

South of Parque Central and separated by a few blocks, the **Mercado Nuevo** (Calle Isabela de Torres and Villanueva, daily

8 am–9 pm) and **Mercado Viejo** (Calle Urena and Separación, daily 8–6:30) are worth a walk around, not only for the possibility of stumbling across a great gift but also to feel the pulse of Dominican life. The former is a cluttered building of stalls selling Haitian paintings, T-shirts, cigars and other typical souvenirs, whose owners are often prepared to bargain prices. The latter, where prices are fixed, is more for locals, selling hardware and household goods, but there is also an interesting *botánica*, or shop selling **religious items** like icons, pictures and candles.

On the eastern outskirts of Puerto Plata, bordering the busy Carretera 5, is the **Brugal Rum Bottling Plant** (open Mon–Fri 9–noon, 2–3:30, admission free), where visitors are welcome to look around and even more welcome to buy a bottle to take home. There is no distillery here, and in truth there's nothing thrilling about watching bottles being put into

boxes, but there is a free taste of the finished product for everyone at the end of the tour.

Conveniently located among the all-inclusives at Playa Dorada, the **Plaza Playa Dorada** is a shopping mall full of **classy boutiques** selling jewellery, stylish clothing and home décor items that have visitors dipping in their pockets. The mall also has tour agents, internet access, restaurants and bars, and endless people-watching opportunities. Just half a kilometre west of the entrance to Playa Dorada, a **cigar shop** (called Cuevas y Hermanos Fabricantes de Cigarros (open Mon–Sat noon–10), located beneath the Café Cito, sells some of the best-known brands at factory prices. Customers considering buying a box can smoke one for free, either in the shop or upstairs at the Café Cito. Cigars are sold in boxes of 25 and, while not exactly cheap – prices range from around US$60 to US$100 a box – are appreciably lower than standard retail outlets.

Where to...
Be Entertained

There is plenty of entertainment on the north coast, both day activities and nightlife. Most beach hotels and resorts provide a wide range of watersports and other activities to keep their guests occupied, and there are plenty of organised day trips for those who fancy a change of environment. Discos are enduringly popular and most large resorts have at least one offering international and local hits. Likewise, most big resorts have some form of evening show, while bars and clubs along the coast get customers dancing to the irresistible beat of *merengue* and *bachata*.

DAY TRIPS

If you get bored lying on the beach during the day, you can sign up for one of the many **organised day trips** on offer, such as a **snorkelling** trip to an offshore island or **white-water rafting** in the mountains. They usually include all necessary equipment as well as food and drinks, depending on the excursion. Most hotels have information about what is available, or you can check out the websites of operators listed in Getting Around (▶ 34).

SPORTS

For sports enthusiasts, the north coast of the DR has not only some of the best beaches in the world for **windsurfers** and **kitesurfers**, but also a couple of world class **golf courses** at Playa Dorada (tel: 320 4262) and Playa Grande (tel: 582 0860). As for spectator sports, between November and February there are **baseball games** at the Puerto Plata Baseball Stadium, which is where Circunvalación Sur meets Avenidas Ginebra and Hermanas Mirabal.

BARS AND NIGHTCLUBS

Turning to nightlife, there are plenty of bars in Puerto Plata catering to expats and foreign visitors, among which **Café Cito** (▶ 80) is a good choice for ambient **jazz and blues** music. The Canadian owner also organises a weekly Pub Crawl, which takes guests to five hot spots along the beach between Puerto Plata and Cabarete. For a more Dominican feel to the night, head for **La Barrica**, at Circunvalación Sur 35/Avenida Colón, after midnight (it's usually empty before), order up a *servicio* (a bottle of rum, two Cokes and ice), and let your body move to the music. The clientele here is almost exclusively Dominican, and the place is very dark, but the Latin sounds are hot.

At Playa Dorada Plaza, **Hemingway's Café** also gets packed towards midnight with guests from the nearby all-inclusive resorts listening and dancing to the latest hits from the US and Europe. There's a **live band** on Thursday and Saturday, and **karaoke** on Fridays. Just opposite Hemingway's, in the Paradise Resort, the **Crazy Moon Disco** is open to everyone and plays a mix of Dominican and US music. The crowd tends to be very mixed, in both age and nationality, and there are some sharp movers on the dance floor from 11 pm until the small hours.

Both **Sosúa** and **Cabarete** have their fair share of bars, though those in Sosúa tend to be more laid-back.

The Samaná Peninsula

Getting Your Bearings

The Samaná Peninsula only occupies a small part of the Dominican Republic, measuring little more than 50km (31 miles) in length and 10km (6 miles) in width. Yet its concentration of beautiful landscapes, both in the mountains and on the coast, make it one of the most appealing regions of the entire country, and ideal for a sightseeing drive (► 161). Separated from the mainland of Hispaniola by impassable marshland until the late 19th century, it is geographically and culturally distinct from the rest of the Dominican Republic.

Previous page: Cliffs at Los Haïtises
Right: The attractive Samaná coastline
Below: The promenade at Santa Bárbara de Samaná

At present most visitors to Samaná arrive between January and March to watch the hump-backed whales in the bay (► 90) and then return to their all-inclusive resorts on the north or east coast. The Samaná Peninsula has a few secluded all-inclusives, but has never attracted visitors in the

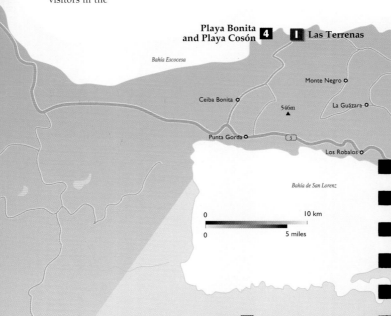

Playa Bonita and Playa Cosón **4**   **1** Las Terrenas

Bahía Escocesa

Monte Negro ○

Ceiba Bonita ○

546m ▲

La Guázara ○

Punta Gorda ○   5

Los Robalos ○

Bahía de San Lorenz

| 0 | 10 km |

| 0 | 5 miles |

5
Parque Nacional Los Haïtises

★ Don't Miss
1. **Las Terrenas** ➤ 88
2. **Whale Watching at Bahía de Samaná** ➤ 90
3. **Playa Rincón** ➤ 93

At Your Leisure
4. Playa Bonita and Playa Cosón ➤ 95
5. Parque Nacional Los Haïtises ➤ 95
6. Santa Bárbara de Samaná ➤ 95
7. Las Galeras ➤ 96

same numbers as Playa Dorada or Punta Cana. However, the construction of an international airport near Samaná and a new highway to Santo Domingo are likely to change all that. In Las Terrenas, the peninsula already has a town that attracts independent travellers in droves, and with fabulous sights such as Salto El Limón (El Limón Waterfall) and Playa Rincón, a beach straight out of a dream, Samaná is sure to feature increasingly on travellers' itineraries.

Playa Rincón 3 *Bahía de Rincón*

7 Las Galeras

○ El Valle

Los Tococnes ○

○ Manuel Chiquito

(5)

Santa Bárbara de Samaná 6 ○ La Palmilla

El Francés ○
○

Cayo Levantado

2
Bahía de Samaná

○ Sabana del Mar

(103)

Chill out in the travellers' town of Las Terrenas,
watch whales at play in Bahía de Samaná and
visit one of the country's best beaches at
Playa Rincón.

Samaná Peninsula in Three Days

Day One

Morning/Afternoon
Settle down on Playa Cacao at **Las Terrenas** (➤ 88) with
a good book and plenty of sun lotion for a day of serious
relaxation. When you get hungry or thirsty, there is a string
of appealing restaurants just a few steps away, among
which Casa Salsa is a good choice.

If you get restless, local tour companies offer **diving**
trips or **horseback rides** to the El Limón Waterfall (above)
or you could even rent a quad (4WD motorbike) and go to
explore nearby beaches such as ➍ **Playa Bonita** (➤ 95).

Evening
Take a stroll round Plaza Taína, Plaza Linda and El Paseo,
three small **shopping malls** in the centre of town, where you
can pick up a few souvenirs. Enjoy a seafood meal on the
beach, then check out the nightlife at Nuevo Mundo nightclub (➤ 100).

Day Two

Morning
If you're here between mid-January and mid-March, join a **2 whale watching tour** around **Bahía de Samaná** (➤ 90), which normally takes a couple of hours, though some tours add other activities, such as a visit to **Cayo Levantado**, making it a full day. Out of season, you can still learn about humpbacks and their habits at the Nature Centre at the western end of Samaná's harbour.

Afternoon
If you're back in time from your trip, explore the small town of **6 Santa Bárbara de Samaná** (➤ 95) – the market, La Churcha and the mysteriously-named "Bridge to Nowhere" (above).

Evening
Enjoy a meal at one of the Malecón's many restaurants, then after a romantic stroll back down the **Malecón** head for a nightclub. At the time of writing, Naomi (➤ 100) was a happening place for dancing.

Day Three

Morning/Afternoon
Take plenty of food and drink with you on this trip, preferably in an ice box, as there are not always vendors on this isolated beach. Follow the coast road **east of Samaná** towards Las Galeras, but turn off left about 10km (6 miles) before Las Galeras to **3 Playa Rincón** (➤ 93), a deliciously deserted piece of paradise. Pass the time as you please – reading a book, snacking on seafood, floating in the limpid waters, revelling in isolation.

Evening
Move on round to **7 Las Galeras** (➤ 96) for a range of restaurants and hotels, and take a romantic stroll along the palm-fringed beach before bed.

ⓘ Las Terrenas

Along with Cabarete, further west along the north coast, Las Terrenas has become hugely popular among independent travellers, mostly due to lots of cheap accommodation, great beaches and friendly locals. In fact some foreign visitors get so hooked on the place they start up businesses here themselves, so that they never have to leave.

The town's first residents back in the 1940s were not so wild about the place. About 30 families were sent here from the suburbs of Santo Domingo by Rafael Trujillo in an effort to get rid of the spreading signs of poverty in the city. No doubt these city dwellers had some difficulty switching to fishing and farming for a living, but somehow they survived and the place developed into one of the busiest fishing villages on the north coast of the peninsula.

Until the 1970s Playa Cacao was unknown to tourism

Independent travellers began to spend time here in the 1970s, no doubt attracted by Playa Cacao, the good swimming beach that fronts the town. In those days, access roads were in poor condition, though now there are sealed roads from Las Terrenas to both Samaná and Sánchez. These days thousands of French, Italians, Germans, Canadians and Brits have moved in, some staying months at a time and making Las Terrenas a mini boom town. This is one of the few places in the country where you will see lots of interaction between locals and foreign visitors.

All a traveller could wish for is concentrated around the centre of Las Terrenas, where the main road from Sánchez meets the beach – bars and restaurants offering Dominican and European drinks and cuisine, a gourmet grocer, shopping malls with Internet cafés and boutiques selling handicrafts, motorbike and quad rental agencies. Quads (4-wheel drive

motorbikes) are extremely popular, as they can go more or less anywhere, including across soft-sand beaches. **Horse riding** around the area is also very popular, diving and windsurfing feature strongly too.

Playa Bonita is one of a number of quiet beaches near Las Terrenas

The main beach in front of town, Playa Cacao, is excellent for swimming as it is protected by a reef about 100m (328 feet) offshore. The reef itself is a reasonable place to go **snorkelling**. If you need a change of scenery, Playa Punta Popy and El Portillo beach to the east, and Playa Las Bellenas, Playa Bonita and Playa Cosón (➤ 95) to the west are all beautiful and also quieter than Playa Cacao.

Las Terrenas makes an ideal base from which to explore the Samaná Peninsula, and trips to Salto El Limón (El Limón Waterfall), Samaná and the beautiful island of Cayo Levantado can be arranged easily through local tour operators (➤ 161). Otherwise you can rent a vehicle and go exploring by yourself. Even if you do not choose to base yourself here, the town is worth visiting for the unique feel that it possesses. After dark, Las Terrenas really comes to life, and nightclubs like Nuevo Mundo keep up the beat till late.

TAKING A BREAK

You are so spoiled for choice of restaurants and bars in Las Terrenas that you could spend hours just choosing a spot. One reliable recommendation is **Brasserie Barrio Latino** (➤ 98), located in El Paseo shopping mall.

🞤 182 C4
✉ 100km (62 miles) northeast of Santo Domingo
✈ Flights into El Portillo Airport from Santo Domingo and Puerto Plata

LAS TERRENAS: INSIDE INFO

Top tip Las Terrenas is at its **most crowded** in July and August, so plan to be there then if you want to party, or pick another time if you want a quiet break.

In more detail For more information about the **Samaná Peninsula**, check out www.samanaonline.com

2 Whale Watching at Bahía de Samaná

For many people, a visit to watch the humpback whales off the Samaná Peninsula is the main reason for holidaying in the Dominican Republic. Though there are many other places worldwide where whale watching is possible, the sheer number that flock into Bahía de Samaná (Samaná Bay) early each year make sightings a certainty. The season runs from mid-January to mid-March, when almost the entire population of North Atlantic humpbacks – more than 10,000 of them! – head for the warm waters of the Caribbean to play, to court and to breed.

After spending the summer roaming the Atlantic in search of food, the whales head south and congregate off the Silver Banks, a large reef about 100km (62 miles) northeast of Puerto Plata. From here many of them make their way into the protected waters of Bahía de Samaná. In the rougher waters of the outer bay, males compete for the attention of the females, while the calm waters of the inner bay provide an ideal nursery for mothers with their newborn calves.

Humpbacks are named for their peculiar way of arching their backs when they dive, and are famed for their fun-loving nature. Scientists studying them find it easy to recognise individuals from the peculiar black and white patterning on their tails – each one is distinct. If you're lucky, you may see the whales **breaching** – somehow getting their entire body out of the water before crashing down again with an almighty splash. They have a varied repertoire of antics, however,

Whale watching has become increasingly popular over the last few years, with more and more boats becoming available

Humpback whale preparing to dive

which also includes lifting the tail and hitting it down on the water, rolling the body and hitting the surface with their long flippers, and diving, when their beautiful tails break the surface in preparation for a descent into the deep.

Male humpbacks communicate with songs that are an odd mix of booms and squeaks. Though generally inaudible above the surface, some tour companies put a microphone below the surface to enable visitors to listen to these eerie sounds. Occasionally, however, the whales perform a trumpet blast on the surface that may be heard from a great distance. It is interesting to note that although the whales' song has been observed to change somewhat during their residence in the bay, the song at the beginning of each season is exactly the same as at the end of the previous one.

Whether these songs and splashing antics are performed purely for fun or are part of a mating ritual is not clear, though during their stay males are constantly vying for the attention of females, who are receptive every two years. A humpback whale's pregnancy lasts about a year, so those conceived one year are born in the same area next year. The mothers use this period of security in Bahía de Samaná to nurse their young and teach them basic survival skills. If you are lucky, you might spot one of the new-born calves, which are light grey in colour.

Growing to around 15m (49 feet) long and weighing in at around 40 tonnes, humpback whales are some of the **largest**

creatures on our planet. Instead of teeth, they have baleen, which filter out shellfish for digestion, and their stomachs have ventral folds for storing huge quantities of food, as well as for displays during mating.

Care must be exercised if our curiosity about these creatures is not to disrupt their migratory routines that have been going on for hundreds of years (The Taínos painted pictures of them on their cave walls long before Columbus arrived). It has become necessary to put restrictions on the proximity to which boats can go in order not to disturb these gentle giants, so you must be patient and hope the whales oblige with an impressive display of splashing while your boat is near.

TAKING A BREAK

If you join a half day tour, on your return you will be conveniently placed on Samaná's Malecón, where several restaurants can serve up a tasty lunch. For a good view of the bay and a change in eating habits, head for **Chino** (➤ 98), a reliable Chinese restaurant with moderate prices located just behind La Churcha.

Close encounters

➕ 182 C3

WHALE WATCHING: INSIDE INFO

Top tips Most tours leave from the harbour at Samaná, last a few hours and cost in the region of US$30–50. Check out the **tour company** and the boat – you might just fry in the sun if the boat has no awning.

• A **reliable tour company** is Victoria Marine, tel: 538 2494, kimbeddall@usa.net

• For fanatics, a few companies organise longer and closer encounters with the whales, including **swimming and snorkelling** near them.

• If you arrive out of season, you can learn about the humpbacks at the **Nature Centre** at the west end of Samaná harbour.

• If you are not interested in joining a tour, you may still catch a glimpse of the whales from the **clifftops** at the extreme end of the peninsula to the east of Samaná.

3 Playa Rincón

Close your eyes and imagine a perfect beach stretching several kilometres, with powdery, cream-coloured sand and turquoise waters. Throw in some towering coconut palms giving shade along its length, and a freshwater river trickling into it at one end. Add a few local people selling fish and cool drinks from an improvised shelter, but no resorts or souvenir stalls, so no crowds of people. Now you have a pretty good image of Playa Rincón, one of the true marvels of the Dominican Republic.

Though there are beautiful beaches all around the coast of the country, nothing quite matches up to Playa Rincón, which has exactly what it takes to make you feel glad to be alive. It is a bit tricky to get to, which is why it is so wonderfully deserted for the most part. From Samaná, follow the highway east towards Las Galeras, but about 10km (6 miles) before the

One of the jewels of the DR, Playa Rincón, the perfect beach

Husking a coconut

town, look for a small turning to the left to Playa Rincón. This weaves its way through a couple of sleepy villages, and the road gets very bumpy for the last few kilometres as you head down through the coconut grove to the beach. If you are lucky, when you arrive, you won't see more than a handful of people on the glorious expanse of sand, though at weekends it can get a bit busier, when Dominicans come and camp overnight.

At the western end of the beach is Río Frío (Cold River) – a shallow, clear stream that runs into the bay and provides an ideal place to freshen up after a swim in the sea's salty water. A narrow track, passable by four-wheel vehicles, weaves between the palms to the eastern end of the bay. This end is even more deserted, and the water is still more tranquil, sheltered as it is by a protruding headland.

For some years, there have been rumours that one of the big hotel chains is going to build a resort here and spoil the tranquil isolation. Yet there was no sign of any impending development at the time of writing, so for now Playa Rincón still offers a dream come true – an idyllic beach for swimming and sunbathing without hordes of other tourists to spoil it.

TAKING A BREAK

At both ends of the beach, there are usually simple food stalls selling fried fish and cold drinks, but it's a good idea to take along some water and snacks, preferably in an ice box, in case they are closed.

➕ 182 C4
✉ 20km (12.5 miles) west of Las Galeras

PLAYA RINCÓN: INSIDE INFO

Top tips The road down to the beach gets very rough for the last stretch, and the soft sand on the beach can be hazardous, so a **4WD vehicle** is the best way to go.

• Though the **coconut palms** provide lovely shade, their falling fruit can be deadly, so don't spread out your towel or park your car beneath one.

• It is also possible to approach Playa Rincón by boat from **Las Galeras**. Enquire at Dive Samaná in Las Galeras (tel: 538 0210).

At Your Leisure

4 Playa Bonita and Playa Cosón

These two beaches, located a few kilometres west of Las Terrenas, are both beautiful, very long and not yet over-run with visitors, so they make ideal spots for a relaxing day by the sea. Both are accessible by dirt tracks leading west from Las Terrenas, and have small hotels and restaurants serving food and drinks. The atmosphere on both beaches is even more relaxed than at Playa Cacao in Las Terrenas, and the colour of the water is more inviting too. Apart from the occasional horse trotting along the beach or an adventurous quad exploring the coast, there is little traffic or activity to disturb sun worshippers on the beach.

182 B4 5km (3 miles) west of Las Terrenas *Guagua* from Las Terrenas

5 Parque Nacional Los Haïtises

Though this national park does not lie within the Samaná Peninsula, most people join a boat tour there from Sánchez, in the southwest corner of the peninsula. The park, bordering the southwest shore of Bahía de Samaná, consists of over 200sq km (78sq miles) of mangrove swamps, rainforest and overgrown limestone outcrops punctuated with caves, some of which were once inhabited by the Taínos (➤ 6). Only a small area of the park is accessible to visitors, and a typical visit includes the caves, Cueva Arena and Cueva de la Línea, where the walls are covered with Taíno petroglyphs depicting people, whales and sharks. Many birds inhabit the area, and you are likely to see pelicans, herons and frigates during the tour. However, keep an eye on the weather, as this area gets more rainfall than most parts of the country.

182 B3 Victoria Marine 538 2494

6 Santa Bárbara de Samaná

Known by everyone simply as Samaná, this town enjoys a lovely location, with snug houses gazing

Taking a boat trip through Parque Nacional Los Haïtises

out over the bay from the verdant hillside. Points of interest include the lively market to the west of town, the tin-roofed La Churcha just off the Malecón, and the Nature Centre (Daily 9–11, 2–5. Admission inexpensive), at the western end of the harbour. La Churcha is the meeting place for what remains of the Afro-American community, and the small Nature Centre provides an interesting overview of local wildlife, including a skeleton of a humpback whale and some fascinating details of its behaviour patterns. Straddling the bay, the curious Bridge to Nowhere, a sturdy concrete structure linking two small islands, Cayo Linares and Cayo Vigia, to the mainland. A huge international marina currently under construction may bring a more cosmopolitan feel to the town when completed.

➕ 182 C4 ✉ Samaná Peninsula
🚌 Bus from Santo Domingo and Puerto Plata

🟦 Las Galeras

Las Galeras is about as laid back as you can get in the Dominican Republic without falling over, so it's the ideal spot for anyone seeking quiet and relaxation. The tiny town only has one street of any signifi-

The beach at Las Galeras sees very few visitors

cance, where most buildings function as restaurants to cater for the steadily growing trickle of visitors. Most people spend their time on the beach, though diving and horse riding are other options. Though several new hotels have been built here in recent years, including a large all-inclusive resort about a kilometre east of town, the atmosphere of Las Galeras remains very relaxed, perhaps because of its remote location in the far northeast of the country. The main focus of attention is the beach, which, while not quite as spectacular as Playa Rincón, is still very pleasant, with regulation coconut palms leaning over a swathe of soft sand. You shouldn't have too much trouble finding a peaceful spot here, but if it is busy around the entrance, walk to the east for a few minutes and you will probably be completely alone. There's not much to do after dark in Las Galeras, but one very loud bar and nightclub, Indiana, does its best to keep the town rocking into the night.

➕ 183 D4 ✉ 32km (20 miles) northeast of Santa Barbara de Samaná
🚌 *Guagua* from Samaná

Where to... Stay

Prices

Expect to pay per double room per night, excluding 22 per cent tax (10 per cent service charge, 12 per cent government tax)

$ under US$50   **$$** US$50–100

$$$ over US$100

LAS GALERAS

Villa Serena $$$

This Victorian-style mansion may not have been designed exclusively for honeymooners, but the 21 plush rooms are so delightfully decorated, and the atmosphere is so serene that the hotel exudes an aura of romance. Each room has a spacious balcony looking across a beautifully landscaped garden to the Atlantic Ocean, where a tiny offshore island sprouts a half dozen palm trees. It is located west of the centre of Las Galeras and has no beach, but there is an attractive pool set in the garden. The staff are super-attentive

and the small restaurant serves up the best food in town, though prices are quite steep.

**➕ 183 D4 ⊠ Calle A, Las Galeras
☎ 538 0000; fax: 538 0009;
www.villaserena.com**

LAS TERRENAS

Casas del Mar Neptunia $–$$

This is a tasteful and good-value budget hotel just 20m (66 feet) from the beach and a short walk east of the centre of Las Terrenas. There are eight spacious bungalows set in a tropical garden with a thatched hut in the centre that serves as restaurant and bar. Rooms

have double doors that open out onto a porch with table and chairs. There are also a couple of large apartments that can sleep up to six people, and the French owner can help organise quad rentals or day trips in the region.

**➕ 182 C4 ⊠ Avenida Emilio
Prud'homme, Las Terrenas
☎ 240 6617; fax: 240 6070;
www.samanaonline.com/
accommodations/htm**

El Portillo Beach Resort
$$–$$$

About 6km (4 miles) east of Las Terrenas between a fabulous beach and a small airstrip, this small all-inclusive resort is very appealing for its competitive prices and relaxed ambience. Rooms in three-floor blocks are surrounded by a jungle of vegetation, and a cluster of villas sits nearer to the beach. The resort offers a range of sports such as kayaking, horse riding and tennis, as well as several excursions in the region. There are five bars,

three restaurants, and a show and dancing every night.

**➕ 182 C4 ⊠ El Portillo, Las Terrenas
☎ 240 6100; fax: 240 6104;
www.portillo-resort.com**

SANTA BÁRBARA DE SAMANÁ

Tropical Lodge $$

The best value of only a handful of places in Samaná, this hotel is situated right on the Malecón to the east of the town centre on the road to Las Galeras. There are great views of the bay, but the location is far enough from the centre to be relaxing. There is a pizzeria, a pool and jacuzzi set in a tropical garden. The 17 rooms are a mix of singles and doubles, some with fans and others with air-conditioning. All bathrooms have hot water. The whole place is immaculately clean and the service is very efficient and attentive.

**➕ 182 C4 ⊠ Malecón, Samaná
☎ 538 2480; fax: 538 2068;
www.tropical-lodge.com**

Where to...
Eat and Drink

Prices

Expect to pay per person for a meal, excluding drinks, tips and tax (22 per cent)
$ under US$2   **$$** US$2–5   **$$$** over US$5

LAS GALERAS

Pescador $$–$$$

Probably the pick of the bunch of restaurants along the main street in Las Galeras, about 500m (550yards) back from the beach. The place is Spanish-run and, as the name suggests, its specialities are seafood in various preparations. The congenial Spanish host can make recommendations as to the day's best choices, and the outdoor patio is a relaxing spot to relax and linger awhile over a cold drink.

⊞ 183 D4 **⊠** Calle Las Galeras, Las Galeras **⊚** 8 am–11:30 pm

LAS TERRENAS

Brasserie Barrio Latino $–$$

Located in a small shopping plaza in the centre of Las Terrenas, this open-air, French-run restaurant is a great find, especially if you're pining for familiar food. The huge menu is available in four languages, and offers filling breakfasts, various salads, pizzas, sandwiches, burgers and steaks, as well as a daily special that is always good value.

⊞ 182 C4 **⊠** El Paseo, Las Terrenas **⊚** 240 6367 **⊚** Daily 7:30 am–midnight (later in high season – Jul–Aug and Dec–Apr)

Havana Café $$–$$$

Located right on the beach in the heart of Las Terrenas, Havana Café manages to be much more than just another restaurant. They serve a good range of salads, soups, steaks and seafood in a classy ambience of bamboo, mahogany and thatch. Set in the courtyard of an attractive shopping mall, Havana Café is a favourite starting point for a night on the town, so it gets pretty lively in the evenings. Saturday night in particular draws a crowd of dancers. Cigars and *merengue* compilation CDs are on sale too.

⊞ 182 C4 **⊠** Plaza Linda, Las Terrenas **⊚** 240 5000 **⊚** Daily 9 am–10 pm (later on Saturdays)

La Salsa $$–$$$

This re-furbished fishing shack on the beach is surrounded by competitors, but keeps drawing in crowds with fantastic seafood and homely Dominican cooking. Its second great strength is the drinks list, which runs to several pages, and

many of the cocktails are served in fresh coconuts. Superb views of swaying palms and azure waters, and the result is romantic and worth the expense.

⊞ 182 C4 **⊠** Calle Playa Cacao, Las Terrenas **⊚** Daily noon–midnight

SANTA BÁRBARA DE SAMANÁ

Chino $–$$

There are several pleasing aspects to discovering this place in Samaná. First of all, Chinese food is not at all common in the DR, so it makes a change. Secondly, not only do they serve a wide range of Chinese dishes, but many typical Dominican dishes too, and prices for everything are reasonable. Perhaps the greatest treat though, is the view of Bahía de Samaná from the terrace, as it is located on a hill behind La Churcha. In summary, Chino is a good choice for either lunch or dinner while in Samaná.

⊞ 182 C4 **⊠** Calle Santa Bárbara, Samaná **⊚** Fri–Wed 11–11

Where to... Shop

While the Samaná Peninsula is not as geared up to tourism as the north and east coasts with their concentrations of all-inclusive resorts, there are still plenty of shopping opportunities. The best variety of products on sale is to be found in Las Terrenas, but Samaná and Las Galeras also have a few boutiques, and the larger hotels and resorts in the region sell souvenirs too. Jewellery, paintings and figurines carved of wood are enduringly popular.

LAS TERRENAS

Despite being a small town, Las Terrenas has three modern shopping malls – El Paseo, Plaza Linda and Plaza Taína – all very near each other in the centre of town, an indication of the town's year-round popularity. **El Paseo** is a two-storey building made largely of wood and set around a plaza with a fountain. Its 40 or so shops include a post office, a bank, a camera shop, a travel agent, a beauty salon and many shops selling works of art and other gifts. Among these, **Galerie El Cacique** has some interesting paintings and reproduction Taíno sculptures; **Blue Corazón** displays jewellery featuring silver, amber and larimar; and **Carib Attitude** sells women's clothes and home décor items.

Almost next door to El Paseo and facing the beach, **Plaza Linda** is a similar mix of boutiques, offices and restaurants. There is a small **amber museum** displaying examples of the precious resin (▶ 26) in various shades, as well as the sky-blue stone called larimar (▶ 54). **Mona Design** is one shop worth browsing around, as it sells lamp stands, mirror frames and furniture made of natural materials such as bamboo and coconut, and can also make objects to order.

Just a few steps away from these two malls, **Plaza Taína** offers more opportunities to pick up attractive gifts among its many shops and boutiques.

Bright **paintings** by Dominican and Haitian artists are a common sight on the streets of all towns in the DR, but Las Terrenas is a particularly good place to look for a painting to take home. This is because there are several artists living locally, both Dominican and foreigners, whose work is on display in galleries. Two places where such work can be found are **Gingerbread** and **Nativ' Arte**, both located on Calle Las Terrenas near the centre of town. Apart from oil paintings and sculptures, these boutiques sell eye-catching artefacts and reproductions of Taíno sculpture. Also on the main road, the **Haitian Art Gallery** features works by some of that country's top artists such as Dabadie, Prosper Louis and Prefete Duffault. The gallery also sells selected brands of cigars, jewellery and beachwear.

SANTA BÁRBARA DE SAMANÁ

The selection of gifts on offer in **Samaná** is more limited than in Las Terrenas, but there are a few shops such as **Indiana Carey Gift Shop**, Malecón Av. 6 (Mon–Sat 9–1, 3–7) and **Etnik Boutique**, Malecón Av. 6 (Mon–Sat 9–noon, 2.30–7) that sell amber and larimar jewellery, home décor items and cigars.

Finally, when you are lounging on the beach you are likely to be approached by wandering vendors selling sunglasses, beach robes, necklaces and beads for braiding hair. They may even offer to braid your hair for you too.

Where to...
Be Entertained

From whale-watching to scuba-diving, from horse-riding to quad safaris, from throbbing nightclubs to campfire sing-songs, the Samaná Peninsula has plenty to keep everyone entertained. Most types of watersports are available, particularly in Las Terrenas, where there is also a kaleidoscope of bars and clubs that stay open until the wee hours.

BY DAY

Many people plan their holiday in the DR around a **whale-watching trip** in Bahía de Samaná (▶ 90), which is limited to the period between mid-January and mid-March and certainly an unmissable

experience if you are here at that time. Yet there are lots of other exciting activities from which to choose. **Scuba diving** to coral reefs and offshore wrecks is organised by Dive Samaná in Las Galeras (tel: 538 0210), who also operate **boat trips** to nearby beaches like Playa Rincón (▶ 93). There are beautiful coral reefs strung all around the peninsula, so **snorkelling** is very popular. **Windsurfing** and **kayaking** are also available on the beach at Las Terrenas. **Tour companies** like Sunshine Services (tel: 240 6164) and Bahía Tours (tel: 240 6088) in Las Terrenas can arrange **catamaran cruises** and various **fishing trips.**

Horse-riding is another popular activity on the peninsula and a

great way to appreciate the region's lush landscapes. Probably the most popular ride is from the village of El Limón to **Salto El Limón** (El Limón Waterfall) (▶ 161), but it's also great fun to ride along the beach. Rancho de la Playa (tel: 240 6501) in Las Terrenas and Rancho Thikis (tel: 223 0035) in Las Galeras are two reliable outfits that rent out horses for around US$10 an hour, and the former even organises horseback treks of several days going deep into the interior.

If you've never ridden a **quad**, or four-wheel motorbike, then an exciting new experience awaits when you rent one or join a **quad safari** organised by the tour companies in Las Terrenas. With their huge wheels and manoeuvrability, they can take you almost anywhere.

BY NIGHT

When it comes to nightlife, **Las Terrenas** is as lively as Cabarete on the north coast with its bars, clubs

and spontaneous beach parties. **Havana Café** (▶ 98) is popular, as is **Nuevo Mundo**, on the main road just south of the town centre. **Indiana Café** and **Paco Cabana**, both located on the beach, are also worth checking out. From Friday to Sunday each week, the Dominican *barrio* south of town hosts a **night market** where food and liquor are on sale and the locals often perform.

Samaná is not such a tourist-oriented town as Las Terrenas, but it is still very lively at night, with **Naomi** on the Malecón and **La Loba** on Avenida Rosario Sánchez drawing crowds at night. The **Ranch Allegre**, also on the Malecón, is an outdoor dance hall playing the latest *merengue* and *bachata* hits. Most people who go to **Las Galeras** are not looking for a raucous nightlife, but rather a tranquil getaway. However, even this small town has a couple of night clubs, of which **Indiana**, on Calle Las Galeras near the centre of town, blasts out Latin music at volume.

Southeast

Getting Your Bearings

The southeast is the largest region of the Dominican Republic, yet it is very sparsely populated and the landscapes are generally undramatic, apart from some spectacular beaches. The main attractions are the all-inclusive resorts that are set on idyllic stretches of coastline, and offshore excursions to islands like the beautiful Isla Saona in the Parque Nacional del Este

Being near to Santo Domingo, Boca Chica gets a constant stream of visitors to its sandy beach, but east of here the countryside gets more rural. San Pedro de Macorís may have seen better days, but it still feels typically Dominican and is the proud birthplace of baseball hero Sammy Sosa (➤ 28). The next town, La Romana, is a jumping off point for snorkelling trips to Isla Catalina (➤ 122), for the nearby Altos de Chavón, and for the Parque Nacional del Este where Taíno pictographs adorn the caves.

There are several all-inclusive resorts around La Romana and Bayahibe, including the enormous Casa de Campo. Yet even this cluster does not compare to the concentration of resorts around Punta Cana and Bávaro, further up the east coast, which receive the highest numbers of visitors in the whole country. For independent travellers brave enough to delve this far into all-inclusive land, the small coastal town of El Cortecito offers the best accommodation options.

Boca Chica **1**   San Pedro de Macorís **2**   Cueva de las Maravillas **5**

Bahía Andrés

Above: A colourful beachside
gallery, Bayahibe
Page 101: The lively beach at
Bávaro

El Cortecito **11**
○ Bávaro

Manati Park **10**

8 Higüey

Punta Cana **9**

3 Altos de Chavón

6
La Romana

7 Bayahibe

*Bahía de
Yuma*

Parque Nacional del Este **4**

Isla Catalina

▲
102m

0 ————————— 20 km
0 ————————— 10 miles

Bahía Catalinita ○ Isla Catalinita

Isla Saona

Rest up on some of the country's most beautiful beaches on the south and east coasts, explore the sleepy towns of San Pedro de Macorís and La Romana, and gaze at Taíno pictographs and petroglyphs in the caves of Parque Nacional del Este.

Southeast in Two Days

Day One

Morning

Cross the Río Ozama (River Ozama) heading east from Santo Domingo on the Autopista Las Americas (Highway 3) and turn off about 30km (19 miles) later at ❶ **Boca Chica**

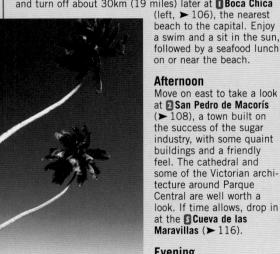

(left, ➤ 106), the nearest beach to the capital. Enjoy a swim and a sit in the sun, followed by a seafood lunch on or near the beach.

Afternoon

Move on east to take a look at ❷ **San Pedro de Macorís** (➤ 108), a town built on the success of the sugar industry, with some quaint buildings and a friendly feel. The cathedral and some of the Victorian architecture around Parque Central are well worth a look. If time allows, drop in at the ❽ **Cueva de las Maravillas** (➤ 116).

Evening

Spend the night at the Santana Beach Resort (➤ 119), about 13km (8 miles) east of San Pedro de Macorís, just 1km (0.6 miles) before the Cueva de las Maravillas. Get your fill of the buffet, have a flutter in the **casino**, take in the **evening show** and check out the nightclub.

Day Two

Morning

Head for **3 Altos de Chavón** (➤ 110), just beyond La
Romana – custom-built in the 1970s in the style of a
medieval Mediterranean village. Here you can take a look
at the excellent **Taíno Museum**, indulge in some splurge
shopping (below), and enjoy a meal overlooking the Río
Chavón (River Chavón). A **boat trip** upriver is yet
another option.

Afternoon

Go down to the port at **7 Bayahibe** (➤ 116) and arrange an
afternoon's exploration of **4 Parque Nacional del Este**
(➤ 113), visiting mangrove estuaries, secluded beaches
and Taíno caves. If you're keen on **snorkelling**, join a trip
to idyllic Isla Saona.

Evening

Eat at the Lebanese-run Shish Kebab Restaurant (➤ 120)
in La Romana. For some good nightlife, go to Club Genesis
in Altos de Chavón (➤ 122).

❶ Boca Chica

Boca Chica has all the requirements of a seaside town: a wide stretch of soft sand; shallow, clear water protected by an offshore reef and shaded by palm trees; plus plenty of bars and restaurants along the front. It is ideal for sun-bathing and swimming, particularly for kids as the water is so calm. There is even a small offshore island, La Matica, to which you can walk out at low tide.

Since there is no beach to speak of in Santo Domingo itself, Boca Chica, located just 30km (19 miles) east of the capital, is the place where city-dwelling Dominicans go to unwind, and there is often a good number of foreigners here too. The town came into being in the mid-19th century as a focus of the **sugar industry**, with large mills all around. When sugar ceased to be a profitable crop, the town declined until President Trujillo built a holiday home here, guaranteeing its popularity for a while. Things got quiet here in the 1980s when the all-inclusive resorts at Playa Dorada and Bávaro began to lure many foreigners away, but with more independent travellers now visiting the country, the future is looking rosy for Boca Chica.

The **Bahía de Andres**, as the bay in front of Boca Chica is known, has a gentle slope that allows you to wade around 100m (328 feet) out from the shore and still be only waist-deep in water. This and other factors like the white sand and proximity of a vast range of refreshments make the place incredibly popular, especially at the weekend.

This popularity has both an up- and a downside. On the one hand, it's a great spot for people-watching. Also, the intense competition for tourist dollars ensures great choices for places to stay and to eat out. Local tour operators also

Above: Relaxing on Boca Chica's magnificent beach
Right: Refreshing coconuts for sale

organise banana boat rides, sailing, snorkelling and even diving trips to a **sunken wreck** at the nearby Parque Nacional Submarino La Cataleta.

On the other hand, since the beach and town get extremely **crowded** at weekends, you might want to plan to be here on a weekday. Even then, when you're trying to relax on the beach, the hawkers and strollers who offer to give you a manicure, braid

your hair, sell you local souvenirs or serenade you with a *mariachi* tune can be annoyingly persistent. The bars in town can be quite lively after dark, but **take care** on the streets as robberies are quite frequent and local prostitutes vie with each other to attract the attention of male visitors.

TAKING A BREAK

For a special treat, make for **Neptuno's Club** (► 120) at the western end of the bay.

➕ 182 B2
✉ 30km (18 miles) east of Santo Domingo
🚍 Express bus from Santo Domingo every 30 mins

BOCA CHICA: INSIDE INFO

Top tips Though finding a good, cheap room is almost impossible in the DR, there are some very reasonably priced alternatives in Boca Chica, such as the **Europa Hotel** (► 119) just a few steps from the beach.
• Boca Chica shares the annual **Merengue Festival** (late July) with Santo Domingo – same musicians but smaller crowds.

2 San Pedro de Macorís

If you're taking a spin round the south coast it is highly recommended that you stop to take a look around the country's fourth largest town. This once grand town has some interesting colonial architecture, colourful local festivals that feature masked dancers, and a reputation for producing baseball stars.

Most of the town's architecture dates back to the early 20th century, and though some of the grand colonial edifices have been renovated to great effect, many are in dire need of some maintenance. One of the first striking buildings you pass on entering town from the west is the **Catedral San Pedro Apostol**, a bold, white, neo-Gothic structure built in 1913. It has an impressive arched doorway and a mahogany altar. Around the church are several other colonial-style buildings, including the former port authority building on Calle Charro, now called the **Centro Cultural Fermoselle**, which displays the work of local artists as well as photographs of bygone days. Other buildings around Parque Central are worth a look, including the eye-catching, cast-iron fire station on Calle Duarte.

More popular than any of these buildings, however, is the **Estadio Tetelo Vargas**, the home of baseball team Estrellas Orientales, located on the north side of town. Most games are

The impressive arched doorway of the Catedral San Pedro Apostol

a sell-out but if you're in town during the season (Oct–Feb), it's worth trying to get hold of a ticket just to experience the electric atmosphere of a game. Among many local boys who have made good in the US Major Leagues, **Sammy Sosa** (➤ 28) is the unrivalled favourite; in fact he is the national sports hero. Though Sammy spends most of his time in the USA, he helped to build a small shopping centre on Avenida Independencia called 30/30, a reference to when he hit 30 home runs and stole 30 bases. A small statue of Sammy ready to bat stands in the entrance to the shopping centre.

If you happen to be here at Christmas or during the **Fiesta de San Pedro** (24–30 June), you might be lucky enough to witness one of the town's stranger scenes. At this time groups of masked dancers called "mummers" go around the streets dressed in bright outfits decorated with feathers and sequins, acting out various colourful dance dramas that recount both stories from the bible and events of local history. The people who perform these dances are "cocolos", the descendants of sugar workers brought from the British Antilles at the beginning of the 20th century.

A snack vendor near the baseball stadium; San Pedro de Macorís has produced some of the finest baseball players in the world

TAKING A BREAK

The **Roby Mar** on Avenida Charro, opposite the cathedral, has great seafood and an intimate atmosphere.

🔳 182 C2

Catedral San Pedro de Apostol
✉ Avenida Charro. 🕒 Daily 8–8.
💰 Free.

Centro Cultural Fermoselle
✉ Avenida Charro and Calle 10 de Septiembre. 🕒 Mon–Sat 9:30–noon, 2–5.
💰 Free

---

3 Altos de Chavón

Located just east of La Romana on a plateau above the Río Chavón (River Chavón), Altos de Chavón is a mock-Mediterranean 16th-century village that was built in the 1970s and now functions both as an artists' community and a tourist attraction. For some it is a delight to discover, while others consider it an amusingly low form of kitsch

The cobbled streets of Altos de Chavón

The site was built at a cost of around US$40 million by Gulf & Western, the company responsible for the enormous Casa de Campo resort next door. It was designed by Italian architect Robert Cappa, who had previous experience in designing movie sets. In fact many visitors get the feeling that they are walking through an elaborate Hollywood set. There's no doubt that the carpenters, stone-masons and other artisans who worked on the project did a good job, because the cobbled streets, coral stone fountains decorated with wrought iron fish and solid buildings made of artificially-aged limestone slabs look as if they have been there for centuries.

There are some striking sights in the village, especially the massive **Greek amphitheatre**, which holds around 5,000 people and has hosted concerts by the likes of Frank Sinatra, Carlos Santana and Gloria Estefan.

The large stage is also ideal for the music and dance extravaganzas that are held here occasionally. The stepped terraces that accommodate the audience offer a good view of the show, and on the hill behind the stage are twelve stone columns that represent the disciples of Christ. If you are lucky, there might be a concert taking place at the time of your visit.

There is also the small but excellent **Museo Arqueológico**, which has probably the best examples and explanations in English of Taíno idols and artefacts anywhere in the country. The display also includes a couple of wonderfully preserved canoes. In the small courtyard of the museum, look out for an unusual tree bearing fruit the size of watermelons. **Iglesia St Stanislaus**, one of the last buildings to be constructed in the village, is still popular for weddings and special events yet seems to creak with age. In front of this church is a fantastic viewpoint from a clifftop down over the Río Chavón, where tour boats offer scenic trips into the interior. Some fancy and expensive restaurants share this lovely river view from their terraces.

Inside an upscale amber sales showroom

Altos de Chavón is also home to a branch of the Parsons School of Design from New York, and both Dominican and foreign students study in this surreal surrounding. Design is an extremely popular subject for Dominicans to study, and

The impressive Greek-style amphitheatre

Galeria Erika's

the national hero in this field is **Oscar de la Renta**, whose exotic outfits are worn by the rich and famous. Though generally based in the USA, de la Renta makes frequent visits to his homeland and his work is occasionally exhibited at Altos de Chavón. His success has enabled him to invest heavily in Dominican tourism, and along with his friend, singer Julio Iglesias, he owns several properties in the southeast, including Punta Cana airport.

Among the shops selling paintings, T-shirts and other souvenirs are art galleries featuring the work of local students, and chic boutiques with dazzling displays of jewellery and Dominican crafts.
Shoppers who would like to browse some gorgeous examples of amber and larimar set in pendants, earrings and bracelets, should take a look in Everett Designs (➤ 121). Be warned, however, that you will have to dig deep if you are tempted to buy any souvenirs, as prices are pitched at the upmarket crowd. There are lots of stylish restaurants here too, serving French, Italian and Mexican food, some with great views down over the river, but prices are a bit on the steep side.

Altos' shops and galleries are full of Dominican arts and crafts

TAKING A BREAK

A meal in **Giacosa**, an upscale restaurant overlooking the Río Chavón, may cost more than average but is an experience to remember. There are many tempting Italian dishes on its menu, and the seafood risotto is particularly delicious.

➕ 183 E2
Museo Arqueológico
🕐 Daily 9:30–5
🎟 Free

Iglesia St Stanislaus
✉ Central square 🕐 Daily 9–7,
Mass Sat–Sun 5 pm

ALTOS DE CHAVÓN: INSIDE INFO

Top tips To find out if there are any upcoming **concerts in the amphitheatre**, check out www.casadecampo.com.do, then click on "enter paradise" and then "what's happening".

• Keep in mind that **the amphitheatre is not sheltered**, so take along an umbrella or sun protection just in case.

• **Altos de Chavón can get crowded** with tour buses during the middle of the day, so if you can choose your time, visit either early or late in the day to appreciate the place without the tourist hordes.

❹ Parque Nacional del Este

The Parque Nacional del Este (Eastern National Park) consists of vast areas of limestone terraces covered with both dry and deciduous forests, as well as cliffs and caves that are decorated with Taíno pictographs and petroglyphs (cave paintings and carvings). There are over a hundred species of birds here, lots of iguanas scuttling about in the undergrowth, and dolphins and manatees in the shallow coastal waters. The park covers over 400sq km (156sq miles), and includes Isla Saona and Isla Catalinita, which are both popular destinations for snorkelling trips

In 1975, the government realised the ecological importance of the extreme southeast of the country, and designated the peninsula and offshore islands as a national park. There are virtually no roads in the territory, so visitors usually explore the national park on a day trip by boat from **Bayahibe** (► 116) or **La Romana** (► 116). Most of these tours head for either Isla Catalinita or Isla Saona for lunch and a *merengue* party, after stopping to snorkel above coral reefs on the way.

The sandy beach of Isla Saona; the island was named after Sabona in Italy

Most boats going to **Isla Saona** make for the sands of Playa Mano Juan, where there are beach chairs and umbrellas, an expensive restaurant run by Club Viva Dominicus (an all-inclusive resort at Bayahibe) and a hiking trail going inland. There are only a couple of tiny fishing villages on the island, so you are unlikely to meet anyone except other tourists on the hiking trails across the island. Other boats stop at the Piscina Natural (natural swimming pool), where a sand bar protects a clear lagoon. If you hire your own boat and want to avoid the crowds, ask the captain to head for the tiny island of Catalinita, where there is good snorkelling, few (if any) tourists, and a chance of glimpsing the magical manatee.

Back on the peninsula, there are some fascinating caves, and if you are prepared to walk for a few kilometres, park rangers can guide you to several interesting spots, such as **Cueva del Puente** or **Cueva José María**, to look at the Taíno pictographs and petroglyphs. The images in the caves show various aspects of Taíno culture and mythology, as well as –historic events like the arrival of Spanish ships. The Cueva José María also has evidence of a 1501 peace treaty with the Spanish, in which the two groups agreed to live in peace. Unfortunately, the peace lasted less than a year before the –systematic extinction of the Taíno people continued.

A friendly face in the shallow waters of the park

In 1997, archaeologists discovered a site called **Manantial de la Aleta**, which was once a place of worship for the Taínos, and consists of a natural well surrounded by four ceremonial plazas. Sadly, this was also the scene of a massacre of Taínos instigated by Nicolás de Ovando in 1503, and bones have been found scattered around the area. At present the site is inaccessible to tourists, though the government plans to open it to the public once excavation work has been completed by experts from the University of Indiana.

If you would like to avoid the crowds, there is an alternative way to enter the national park, from the town of **Boca de Yuma** in the northeast. Just beside the park station here is the **Cueva de Bernardo**, a large, bat-filled cave with Taíno petroglyphs on the wall mingled with modern graffiti. Also at the park station, it is possible to hire a ranger to take you to other caves further inside the park, or to hire a horse to ride along the coastline, or even to arrange a fishing trip in the channel between Isla Saona and the mainland.

TAKING A BREAK

If you go on an organised tour into the park, lunch is usually provided, but if you hire your own boat, pick up a take-away lunch and drinks in Bayahibe or La Romana before leaving.

➕ 183 E1
🕘 Daily 8–6
🎫 Moderate

PARQUE NACIONAL DEL ESTE: INSIDE INFO

Top tips If you plan to explore the caves of Parque del Este make sure you have plenty of **insect repellent**, as wasps and sandflies can be a major irritation. Also, don't forget to wear sturdy walking shoes and take along a good torch.
• **Check out the itinerary** of the boat tour carefully, as some trips are nothing more than a mobile drinking and dancing party.

Beach huts on
Isla Saona

At Your Leisure

5 Cueva de las Maravillas

It is certainly worth seeing some Taíno paintings and carvings while in the Dominican Republic, and this cave, just north of Highway 3 on the road east of San Pedro de Macorís presents as good an opportunity as any. Though discovered in 1926, this deep cave has only recently been opened to the public. A state-of-the-art lighting system in the cave illuminates each area as you come to it, then dims again as you pass, and there is a lift for easier disabled access. There are lots of Taíno pictographs that resemble cartoons, but unfortunately lots of modern graffiti too, and stalactites that have been broken off to sell to tourists. A small museum relating to Taíno culture will open in one section of the cave in the near future.

➕ 183 D2 ✉ North of Highway 3, 14km (8 miles) east of San Pedro de Macorís and just beyond the entrance to Santana Beach Resort ⏰ Tue–Sun 9–5 💰 Moderate

The quiet fishing village of Bayahibe

6 La Romana

Originally founded by the Spanish in 1502, La Romana became one of the key towns of the sugar industry in the early 20th century. It still prospers from this industry, though the presence of nearby tourist attractions like the enormous Casa de Campo Resort and Altos de Chavón (➤ 110) now help to swell the town's coffers. Casa de Campo is the big daddy of all-inclusives, with its own private airport, fourteen swimming pools and nine restaurants. There are no tourist attractions as such within La Romana, but the colourfully-painted shops and friendly people make it worth taking a stroll around the town centre.

➕ 183 D2 ✉ 37km (23 miles) east of San Pedro de Macorís

7 Bayahibe

Until recently, Bayahibe was a quaint and quiet fishing village that made a great spot to hang out for independent travellers. Now, however, the construction of several all-inclusive resorts to both the east and west of town has robbed the area of its best beaches. Bayahibe remains the main port for boat trips into the national park (especially to Isla Saona), and although most visitors just pass through, a pleasant hour could be spent in one of the seafront cafés, watching the waterborne action in the port.

183 E1 55km (34 miles) southeast of San Pedro de Macorís Boats to Parque Nacional del Este

8 Higüey

After San Pedro de Macorís and La Romana, Higüey is the only other town of any size in the southeast of the country. Its streets are unattractive and it could easily be given a miss were it not for the existence of the Basílica de Nuestra Señora de Altagracia, the country's most important religious site. The basilica houses a much-venerated, 16th-century portrait of the Virgin of Altagracia, which is believed to bring about miraculous cures, and if you happen to be near here on 21 January or 16 August, you will see pilgrims from all over the country arriving to participate in processions and to pay their respects to the holy image. Though the architectural merit of its modernist style is debatable, the 80m-high (262 feet) concrete arch is certainly striking. Inside, the stained glass windows, hundreds of flickering candles and praying supplicants create a pious atmosphere.

183 E2 154km (96 miles) east of Santo Domingo

9 Punta Cana

The east coast of the DR has some of the country's most perfect beaches, and receives around 1 million visitors a year. Almost all of them arrive at the Punta Cana International Airport and spend their time within the grounds of one of the many all-inclusive resorts which spread along 30km (19 miles) of the coast from Punta Cana to Bávaro. Though all-inclusive resorts can be found all over the country, those on the east coast seem to do a better job than those in other regions in the sense that they offer more options for eating, and a wider range of activities. This may have developed out of necessity, given the fact that there are no other real attractions on the east coast. Thus it is possible in most resorts to sign up for deep sea fishing trips, scuba diving, horse riding and jeep excursions, as well as beach and watersports like kayaking and parasailing.

183 F2 45km (28 miles) east of Higüey

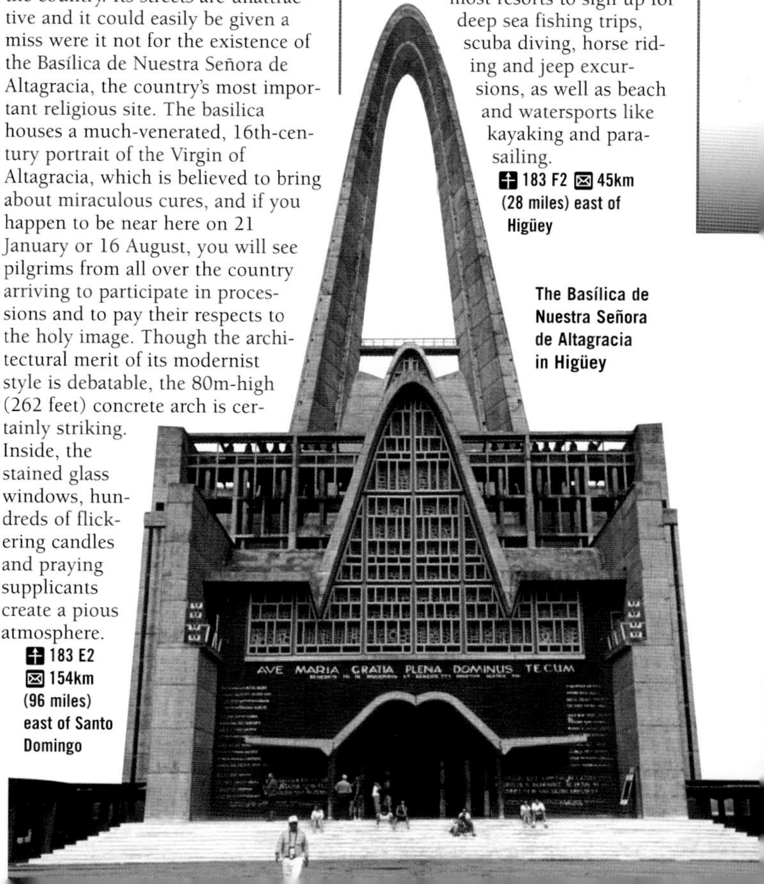
AVE MARIA GRATIA PLENA DOMINUS TECUM

The Basílica de Nuestra Señora de Altagracia in Higüey

🔟 Manati Park

The line-up of entertainment here sounds great – sea lion and dolphin shows, dancing horses, acrobats on horseback, a parrot show, and Taíno dancing; plus turtles, crocodiles, flamingos, sharks and stingrays (but no manatees). There is no shortage of visitors either, probably due to the park's clever location near the all-inclusive resorts at Punta Cana and Bávaro. Yet the entrance fee is quite high (US$25, US$15 for kids) and if you want to swim with the dolphins or watch the dancing horses, you'll have to pay much more. Needless to say, in a theme park like this, there are plenty of opportunities to eat, drink and shop. However, animal rights groups have constantly criticised the park since its opening in

1997 for its inhumane treatment of animals, particularly the dolphins, several of which have died, so deciding whether to go might be a dilemma for some.

➕ 183 F2 ✉ Carretera Manati, Bávaro
🕐 Daily 9–6; for show times visit
www.manatipark.com 🅿 Expensive

🔟 El Cortecito

Located just north of the all-inclusives at Bávaro, this small town has sprung up quickly in recent years, catering to Dominican holidaymakers and independent foreign travellers. It has a real seaside atmosphere, with colourful shops selling postcards, beach gear and Dominican handicrafts. The long, sandy beach can get quite busy in front of town, with all kinds of water sports on offer, but a ten-minute stroll away from the centre should land you in a personal paradise, far from the crowds. There are a few basic but clean hotels to choose from and a good range of restaurants, including the hugely popular Capitán Cook seafood restaurant right on the front (➤ 120).

➕ 183 F2 ✉ 57km (36 miles) east of Higüey

Above: Higüey's (➤ 117) large central market is always a hive of activity
Left: Parrots at Manati Park

Where to... Stay

Prices

Expect to pay per person for a meal, excluding drinks, tips and tax (22 per cent)

$ under US$50 **$$** US$50–100 **$$$** over US$100

BAYAHIBE

Cabaña Elke $$

This is a small, Italian-run hotel 5km (3 miles) east of Bayahibe, next to the Club Viva Dominicus all-inclusive resort. It has nine standard rooms with double beds, fans and hot-water bathrooms, and another nine larger rooms which have lounges, some even with kitchens. Guests are allowed to use the restaurants, beach and extensive facilities at the neighbouring resort. There are some good sea views, and the service is friendly and efficient.

➕ 183 E1 ⬛ Zona Dominicus, Bayahibe ☎ 696 0148; www.viwi.it/turvillaggio.htm

BOCA CHICA

Europa $–$$

The greatest difficulty for budget travellers in the DR is the general lack of decent inexpensive accommodation, but fortunately there are a few exceptions. Along with Cabarete and Las Terrenas, Boca Chica has several cheap hotels, of which this is the pick of the bunch. It has 33 rooms that are all different, ranging from singles with fans to superior air-conditioned rooms that can sleep up to six, with continental breakfast included.

➕ 182 B2 ⬛ Calle Dominguez, on the corner of Avenida Duarte ☎ 523 5721; fax: 523 6994

EL CORTECITO

El Cortecito Inn $$

The east coast around Punta Cana and Bávaro has some of the country's best beaches, but is mostly dominated by all-inclusive resorts. If you'd like to take a look at these powder-soft stretches of sand, your best bet is to head for the small town of El Cortecito, where the local beach is as good as it gets, and very popular among Dominicans. This 67 room hotel has a small swimming pool and is convenient to the beach, shops and restaurants.

➕ 183 F3 ⬛ Calle Playa, El Cortecito ☎ 552 0639; fax: 552 0641

LA ROMANA

Casa de Campo $$$

Casa de Campo is the mother of all-inclusive resorts in the DR, occupying a massive 2,800 ha (6,900 acres) of coast just southeast of La Romana. It boasts an impressive range of facilities – 14 swimming pools, 2 golf courses, a 24-hour tennis centre, shooting, horse-riding, polo training and a beauty spa, among others. As you might expect this is the choice of the rich and famous. The regular rooms are very spacious, and the private villas come with a butler, maid and private chef.

➕ 183 D2 ⬛ Off Highway 4, just east of La Romana ☎ 523 3333; fax: 523 8548; www.casadecampo.com

SAN PEDRO DE MACORÍS

Santana Beach Resort $$$

Set on an isolated part of the coast between San Pedro de Macoris and La Romana, this all-inclusive resort has very tasteful two-storey villas and thoughtfully laid-out gardens, as well as an excellent beach. There are four restaurants, several bars, and a casino

➕ 182 C2 ⬛ Just south of Highway 4, 13km (8 miles) east of San Pedro de Macoris ☎ 412 1010; fax: 412 1818; www.playasantana.com

Where to...
Eat and Drink

Prices
Expect to pay per person for a meal, excluding drinks, tips and tax (22 per cent)
$ under US$2 $$ US$2–5 $$$ over US$5

BAYAHIBE

Supercafeteria Julissa $–$$

If you get hungry or thirsty while in Bayahibe, you could do worse than drop into this place, which, despite its grand-sounding name, is a simple, open-sided restaurant near the beach. They serve good, filling breakfasts – American, European and local – a wide variety of sandwiches and all kinds of fruit juices at competitive prices; in the evening the bar prepares ice-cold daiquiris and a range of cocktails.

➕ 183 E1 ⊠ Malecón, Bayahibe
🕐 Daily morning–late evening

BOCA CHICA

Neptuno's Club $$$

This lovely old wooden building sits out over the water at Boca Chica, and glass panels enable diners to watch manta rays and sharks swimming below in an enclosed area. Moored at the restaurant's jetty is a small replica of the *Santa María*, Columbus' boat of discovery, which now houses a lively bar. Given the fantastic view across the bay and its great range of dishes on offer (with seafood the speciality), it is hardly surprising that this place is extremely popular. Better to make reservations to avoid disappointment.

➕ 182 B2 ⊠ Avenida Duarte 12, Boca Chica ☎ 523 4703 🕐 Daily lunch and dinner

EL CORTECITO

Capitán Cook $$–$$$

Located on the beach at El Cortecito near Bavaro, this seafood restaurant has earned fame nationwide for its terrific food. There is an indoor dining area as well as a large shaded area on the beach where you can wiggle your toes in the soft sand. On entering, patrons have to walk past the grill where the aroma of prawns and lobsters makes your mouth water. All seafood is on display and prices are quoted per kilo. Because of its popularity, Capitán Cook is often full, so it's best to make a reservation, particularly if you are in a group.

➕ 183 F3 ⊠ Calle Playa, El Cortecito ☎ 552 0645 🕐 Daily lunch and dinner

LA ROMANA

Shish Kebab $–$$

There are not too many outlets for Middle Eastern food in the Dominican Republic, but this little gem in La Romana is worth seeking out for its intriguing dishes and great quality. Some examples are *warak-inab* (stuffed grape leaves) and *baba ghanoush* (a spicy eggplant dip). Other Middle Eastern dishes include *mezze*, or a selection of hors-d'oeuvres-like dishes, chicken kebab with tahini sauce, hummus, falafel and good pitta bread. They also serve international dishes like pepper steak, pizza and grilled fish, and their prices are very reasonable. Although Shish Kebab may specialise in Middle Eastern food, rest assured, alcoholic beverages like rum are available as well as a reasonable selection of wines.

➕ 183 D2 ⊠ Calle Creales, La Romana ☎ 556 2737 🕐 Daily lunch and dinner

Where to... Shop

As with the rest of the Dominican Republic, the most typical souvenirs to buy on the southeast coast are jewellery set with amber (▶ 26) and larimar (▶ 54), Haitian and Dominican paintings, cigars and rum, and CDs of *merengue* and *bachata* music. However, at the beach resorts you may be tempted to pick up some beachwear, such as a colourful parasol, a new swimsuit or a hat to shade you from the fierce sun.

The **all-inclusive resorts** of the region have their own gift shops that usually stock a range of typical souvenirs, though the choice may be limited and prices tend to be

somewhat inflated. Therefore if you are travelling around the region, it is worth browsing the local shops and markets, where you may find a bargain. In the popular resort areas, there are also wandering beach vendors selling trinkets like necklaces and bracelets.

Probably the best selection of Dominican arts and crafts on sale is to be found at **Altos de Chavón** (▶ 110), where the imitation medieval village is full of art galleries, jewellery boutiques and souvenir shops. To see a magnificent display of **designer jewellery** featuring amber and larimar, have a browse in **Everett Designs**, where the qualities of these precious stones are shown off at their best. However, be prepared to dig deep in your pockets if you feel the urge to possess a piece come over you, as prices here are expensive. In fact this is true for all shops in the village. The shop owners seem to reason that many visitors are here only a few days and since this is their

only real shopping opportunity, they will buy whatever the price. As always, it pays to look around and compare prices before making a choice.

One unique feature of Altos de Chavón is that it hosts a resident community of artists and designers who study here, and their work is on display in several **art galleries** in the village. If you fancy yourself as a connoisseur of fine art, you might pick up a painting by a future Picasso here at a relatively give-away price.

If you are staying in the all-inclusives at **Punta Cana** or **Bávaro** and get the urge to shop, head for **Bávaro Plaza**, just north of the all-inclusive resorts. This single-storey shopping mall is geared to tourists, and is a maze of shops selling clothes, jewellery, paintings and other arts and crafts. If you are travelling independently and staying at **El Cortecito**, the main street behind the beach has shops selling souvenirs and postcards.

SAN PEDRO DE MACORÍS

Roby Mar $$$

Conveniently situated just across the road from the cathedral in San Pedro de Macorís, this is the town's best restaurant. As might be expected, the speciality is seafood, and during the day local fishermen sell their catch from stalls in front of the restaurant. Depending on the catch, there can be a fine selection of lobster, squid, octopus, king crabs and a wide range of fish from barracuda to swordfish. The atmosphere, particularly in the evening, is very romantic, with candlelit tables set out by the river. The wine list isn't particularly long or sophisticated, but there are ice cold rum cocktails and light, refreshing beer which goes well with the seafood. Considering this ambience, prices are reasonable.

🚌 182 C2 ⊠ Avenida Charro, San Pedro de Macorís ⓒ Daily lunch and dinner

Where to...
Be Entertained

The fact that the southeast attracts the greatest number of tourists in the entire Dominican Republic (most of them to Punta Cana and Bávaro) means that there is plenty to do both in the day and at night. Watersports like snorkelling, diving, swimming and windsurfing keep most people occupied during the day, though most resorts also offer day trips to various places of interest in the region. The main activities at night are dining, drinking and dancing, either in the numerous well-appointed all-inclusive resorts or at bars and restaurants in the local towns of San Pedro de Macoris and La Romana.

DAY TRIPS

While it's possible to make long **day excursions** into the capital, Santo Domingo, to do some sight-seeing and shopping, a more popular day out is to hop aboard a boat and go **snorkelling at Isla Saona** or **Isla Catalina** Boats leave from La Romana and Bayahibe, and one reliable company that operates such tours (out of La Romana) is Flamingo Bay (tel: 554 2301; flaminhgobay@codetel.net.do), whose glass-bottomed boats head out to the beautiful reefs around Isla Catalina.

DIVING

There's plenty of good **scuba diving** in the southeast too, especially around Boca Chica, where Orca Divers (tel: 323 5369) organise trips to nearby Parque Nacional Submarina La Caleta which has some **shipwrecks** to explore. Just off Isla Catalina near La Romana is a spectacular dive site called simply "the Wall", where a marvellously-preserved reef teems with colourful life. Trips there are organised by Circe Divers (tel: 246 3115), based at Casa de Campo (▶ 119).

NIGHTLIFE

All-inclusive resorts go out of their way to make sure that their guests have plenty of alternatives, from **live shows** and **nightclubs** to free booze in all the bars and **cable TV** in the rooms. If you're staying in the Punta Cana/Bávaro area, **Caribe Caliente**, a nightly music and dance performance in the Parque Tematico La Hispaniola (tel: 552 6262, admission expensive) near Bávaro, is a feast for the eyes, and guests are invited to join the show's cast at their intimate night-club after the show. The **Greek amphitheatre** at **Altos de Chavón** (▶ 110) also hosts shows by international and Dominican entertainers.

Nightclubs in the resorts tend to play music that is familiar to visitors from afar, but the Dominican DJs are so proud of their music that they are bound to mix in a few *merengue* and *bachata* songs. The result tends to be a mix of current international pop music hits and well-known local standbys. For a stronger dose of authentic Dominican music, head for one of the clubs in **San Pedro de Macoris** or **La Romana**. In San Pedro, Lexus and Café Caribe, both located near the western end of the Malecón, draw lots of locals, while in La Romana, check out La Fava night-club on Calle Gonzalvo near Parque Central. In **Altos de Chavón**, one of the most popular haunts at night is Club Genesis close to the Casa de Campo.

Southwest

Getting Your Bearings

The southwest is the least visited region of the Dominican Republic, but has plenty to offer adventurous types. The terrain varies from bone-dry desert to lush mountains, inland lakes, and some superb beaches, even if they are a bit stony.

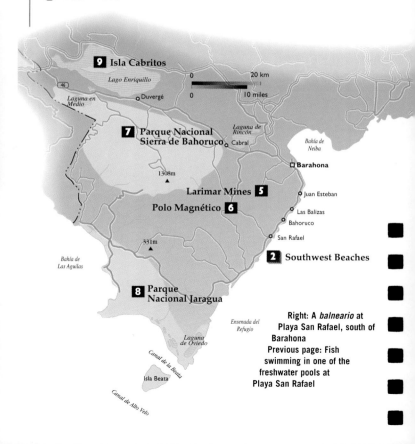

Right: A *balneario* at Playa San Rafael, south of Barahona
Previous page: Fish swimming in one of the freshwater pools at Playa San Rafael

There is an attractive area of sand dunes and salt flats near Baní, while the country's only larimar mines are located near Barahona. Also near Barahona, there is a "magnetic pole", where the effects of gravity appear to be reversed. One interesting option in the region is to drive around Lago Enriquillo (► 164), where you are likely to see wildlife such as iguanas, crocodiles and flamingoes.

There are few tourist attractions in the main towns of the region – San Cristóbal, Baní, Azua and Barahona – but as with the rest of the country, the locals are friendly and welcoming. Few people speak English in these parts and the roads can be rough, but these hardships bring rewards. You can be sure that you will run into hardly any other tourists and you will get a real sense of discovery as you explore the region's beaches, national parks and remote habitations near the Haitian border.

Above: Choosing the perfect orange in Baní's fruit market

Presa de Valdesia

San Cristóbal
3

Bahía de Ocoa

Bahía de Najaya

(2)

4 Baní

I Las Salinas

Explore the sand dunes and salt flats near Baní
and relax on a string of superb beaches
south of Barahona.

Southwest in Two Days

Day One

Morning/Lunch

Head west out of Santo
Domingo on Highway 2
towards **3 San Cristóbal**
(below, right ➤ 132). It
was on this highway that
Trujillo's dictatorship
came to an end in 1961
after a carefully planned
assassination. Pause for a
look at the cathedral in
San Cristóbal, then move
on to **4 Baní** (➤ 132),
where you will come
across some colourfully
painted houses. Follow
the coast road 16km (10
miles) southwest of Baní
to **1 Las Salinas** (➤ 128)
to check out the sand
dunes, salt flats and a
white sand beach. Linger
over lunch at the Salinas
Hotel (➤ 135).

Afternoon

Return to Baní and con-
tinue west on Highway 2
through Azua de
Compostela, then branch left on Highway 44 to Barahona
(above), the region's main town. The roadside vegetation
varies from arid and barren to lush and prolific as the
route climbs over mountains and follows river valleys.

Evening

If you're not quite ready to rest up in your hotel yet,
explore the local nightclubs in Barahona. In-places include
Lotus and Legends (➤ 138)

Day Two

Morning/Afternoon

Drive down the coast road from Barahona (Highway 44) and pick your favourite of the **2 southwest beaches** (above ➤ 130) from Quemaito, Bahoruco, San Rafael, Paraíso or Los Patos. Each beach has its own character and they are all within easy reach of each other. Settle down for a day of relaxation – swimming in the sea, cooling off in the *balnearios* (natural pools) and snacking on seafood.

If you are feeling energetic, go and explore the only **5 larimar mines** in the world (➤ 133).

Or, if you're in the mood for something more adventurous than kicking back on a beach, spend the day driving round **Lago Enriquillo** (➤ 164), a journey of about 200km (124 miles) that fills a day nicely. The route passes some of the country's most famous Taíno petroglyphs and you might also catch sightings of iguanas, crocodiles and flamingoes on the lake.

Evening

Settle in for dinner at your hotel or search out another beachfront alternative, such as Brisas del Caribe (➤ 136) in Barahona.

① Las Salinas

Las Salinas, located at the end of a peninsula that curls round like a finger beckoning, rewards curious adventurers with the sensuous curves of the Baní sand dunes and the surreal pastel complexions of the salt pans. There is also a good windsurfing beach here and boat trips around the Bahía de las Calderas can be arranged. The skies are almost always sunny, so it's a great place to go for a suntan.

A visit to this remote area involves a diversion from the main road to Barahona, following the coast road southwest about 20km (12 miles) from **Baní** to Las Calderas and then Punta Salinas, an area that has a very unusual climate and landscape. Like much of the southwest, this region is very dry – so dry in fact that the sun shines almost every day of the year. The result is the highest sand dunes in the Caribbean and a huge area of salt flats that jut out into the sea.

To reach the sand dunes, you have to enter a naval base and follow the road to the left. The dunes stretch for an area

A striking view of the Bahía de las Calderas from the Salinas Hotel

of over 20sq km (8sq miles), and there are plenty of places where you can pull up at the roadside and clamber up a high dune for an overview. While this may not be the Sahara Desert, if you have never been in an area of **dunes** before it can be very impressive. The fine sand is in constant motion, creating rippling lines up the slopes of the dunes, and only a few hardy shrubs can survive in this harsh terrain.

The **salt flats** consist of huge pans of shallow water, each a slightly different pastel shade of blue, purple or green, with mounds of salt piled up at their edges. Workers – mostly Haitians – toil in the searing sun to fill flat wooden rafts with salt from the pans, then tow them to the edge and shovel off the heavy content. Just watching the effort involved is enough to make you feel faint, and the brightness of the heaps of salt is quite dazzling to the eyes.

Las Salinas itself consists of nothing more than a small cluster of houses, but the Salinas Hotel (➤ 135) is a good place either to stay overnight or stop for a meal. Its breezy terrace looks out over a pool to Bahía de las Calderas and the congenial staff can help arrange diving or snorkelling trips. The white sand beach here also attracts windsurfers, as the bay usually gets a good breeze. Punta Salinas has already become a popular weekend getaway for Dominicans from the capital, but has only recently become a destination for more adventurous foreign visitors.

TAKING A BREAK

The **Salinas Hotel** (➤ 135) has a varied menu and reasonable prices.

➕ 181 E1
✉ 95km (60 miles) west of Santo Domingo

LAS SALINAS: INSIDE INFO

Top tips Climbing up the sand dunes is best done early or late in the day, otherwise **the sand can be roasting**.

• The rippling patterns in the sand dunes and the pastel-coloured salt flats present great opportunities for some striking **abstract photography**.

2 Southwest Beaches

As with most other regions of the DR, the main attractions of the southwest are its beaches, though they are quite different to those in the rest of the country. The verdant mountains of the Sierra Bahoruco drop down steeply to the coast, providing a lush green background, while a narrow road winds along the coast, revealing fantastic views of the beaches from high elevations.

There is no beach to speak of in Barahona, but after following Highway 44 south of town for around 6km (4 miles), **Playa Quemaito** beckons on the left. The swaying palms, turquoise waters and partly-sandy beach give it a classically inviting appearance. It is particularly good for children to swim here, as the beach is protected by a coral reef offshore. There are no big hotels here either, so it is rarely crowded in midweek, though it can get busy with locals from Barahona at the weekend.

The next village south is Arroyo, from where a dirt road leads up into the hills to the **larimar mines** (➤ 133). After this comes the fishing village of **Bahoruco**, where a stony beach stretches for several kilometres and the region's only all-inclusive resort enjoys tranquil isolation.

The most striking beaches are the next few south of Bahoruco, beginning with **Playa San Rafael**, which is very popular with Dominicans at the weekends. The secret of its popularity is the freshwater stream that tumbles down the mountain and emerges at the end of the beach, forming a *balneario*, or natural swimming pool, that provides an ideal spot to freshen up after frollicking in the sea. There are bathrooms

The lush green interior gives way to clear coastal waters

Larimar: The Cool Blue Stone

The semiprecious stone called larimar is unique to the Dominican Republic, and the only mines here are in the southwest. In contrast to amber's warm tones, larimar is most commonly a shade of pale blue reminiscent of a clear ocean or a cloudless sky, though it can vary from almost white to a rich turquoise. Apart from being beautiful to look at, larimar is also reputed to have a calming effect on the wearer. The larimar museum in Santo Domingo (➤ 54) has some wonderful examples on display.

nearby the beach as well as food stalls selling freshly grilled seafood, not to mention a fantastic view back down over the beach from a promontory just beyond San Rafael.

The next two beaches down the coast are **Paraíso** and **Los Patos**, both of which are also very popular among Dominicans at the weekend. Though Paraíso does have a few palm trees leaning towards the crashing surf and some patches of sand, the beach is often littered with rubbish. Los Patos, on the other hand, has a convenient freshwater lagoon that is even more popular than the *balneario* at San Rafael, attracting hundreds of visitors to its cool waters. There are no attractive beaches beyond Los Patos, so when you've had a look around here, head back up the coast to spend a few hours on the beach of your choosing.

TAKING A BREAK

There are food stalls that offer grilled or fried chicken or fish and sometimes goat stew. If you are looking for a proper restaurant, the **Pula**, opposite the church in Los Patos, serves several seafood dishes in Italian or Dominican style.

The swaying palms of Playa Quemaito

✚ 183 F5

At Your Leisure

3 San Cristóbal

San Cristóbal's greatest claim to fame is as the birthplace of President Trujillo, though it is hardly surprising that there are no memorials in town to the dictator. It is basically a busy industrial town with little of interest to tourists, though it is worth stopping at the cathedral by the square in the centre of town. Trujillo spent millions of dollars of government money renovating this grand, mustard-coloured edifice, and its walls are lined with detailed murals by the Spanish painter Zanetti, who fled to the DR during the Spanish Civil War (1936–39). Trujillo lived in the Casa de Caoba (Mahogany House) on a hill a few kilometres north of town, and there are plans to open it to the public at some future date. Near the house is the Balneario La Toma, once El Generalísimo's private spring baths, but now open to the public.

➕ 181 F1

The church at San Cristóbal

Balneario La Toma
🕐 Mon–Fri 9–6 💲 Inexpensive

4 Baní

Many of the simple wooden houses in Baní are painted in delightful combinations of harmonising pastel shades – a typical Dominican trait that gives the country a real tropical flavour. The town was settled by immigrants from the Canary Islands in the 18th century when the Spanish were worried about a French invasion. The population prospered, thanks to local resources such as mahogany and salt. The town's most illustrious resident was General Máximo Gómez, who helped to lead the resistance against the Spanish in Cuba from 1868 to 1878 that led to independence. You can visit his birthplace, but there is little to see apart from a bust of the general and a solitary post of his former home.

Scene at the market in Baní

From May to July, look out for the small, sweet mangoes for which Baní is famous and, if you happen to be there from 15–24 June, join in the celebrations of the *fiesta patronal* (➤ 13) in honour of San Juan Bautista, when Baní quakes with dancing, singing and loud Afro-Latino music.

🞣 181 F1

Casa de Máximo Gómez
🕐 Mon–Sat 9–5
🎫 Free

❺ Larimar Mines

To witness larimar (➤ 131) being extracted from the earth, turn inland at the small village of Arroyo between Playa Quemaito and Playa Bahoruco on Highway 44 south of Barahona, and follow a rough road for about 8km (5 miles) west into the hills towards the village of José Joaquin. The mines themselves are nothing special, but if you arrive when miners are descending or ascending the scant wooden frames, their agility will impress you. The mines are occasionally closed, so check with your hotel before heading up there. In this area, locals offer small pieces of unpolished stone for sale at the roadside.

🞣 183 F5 ✉ near José Joaquin, southwest of Barahona

❻ Polo Magnético

If you're someone who is fascinated by apparent contradictions in the laws of physics, take a drive to the village of Polo, which is easiest accessed via Cabral, northwest of Barahona. Right beside the road, a billboard indicates the *Polo Magnéticc* (Magnetic Pole), where you can pull off at a right fork, leave your car in neutral, and watch it

Fresh fruits abound

being drawn uphill. Any round object placed on the road produces the same effect, but nobody is quite sure why.

➕ 183 F5 ✉ Cabral, northwest of Barahona

❼ Parque Nacional Sierra de Bahoruco

This national park covers 800sq km (312sq miles) and lies to the west of Barahona and south of Lago Enriquillo. It consists mostly of inaccessible mountains, some of which are over 2,000m (6,560 feet) high and covered with lush rainforest. Other parts of the park are completely arid. Few people explore this area thoroughly as there is nowhere to stay at night and the roads are very poor, but it can make an exciting day's adventure in a 4WD vehicle (➤ 164). The entrance to the park is south of Duverge, where you can drive up to the Loma de los Pinos and a lookout point called El Acetillar.

➕ 180 B1 ⏰ Daily 8–5 💵 Inexpensive

❽ Parque Nacional Jaragua

At 1,400sq km (546sq miles), this is the largest national park in the country, though it is visited infrequently due to its remote location. It occupies the southernmost peninsula of Hispaniola and includes the large Isla Beata and the Laguna de Oviedo. The latter is home to a large population of flamingoes for much of the year,

and it is possible to take a boat ride on the lake to see them and other exotic birds such as pelicans and buzzards. If you have use of a 4WD vehicle, you could head for Bahia de las Aguillas (Bay of the Eagles) near Cabo Rojo, which some consider to be the country's finest beach. The region is very dry and is characterised by huge cacti, while some of its caves contain Taíno petroglyphs and pictographs.

➕ 183 E4 ⏰ Daily 8–5 💵 Inexpensive

❾ Isla Cabritos

Located in the middle of Lago Enriquillo, Isla Cabritos is inhabited by American crocodiles, flamingoes and iguanas, which make it a popular place to visit. Boats sail to the island from the north shore of Lago Enriquillo, about 4km (2.5 miles) east of La Descubierta. Tours tend to leave early in the morning, so you will need to make a very early start from Barahona or stay the night in basic accommodation at La Descubierta. The island is all below sea level and covered with cacti and other desert plants. The iguanas here are virtually tame and always on the lookout for snacks.

➕ 180 A1 ✉ Lago Enriquillo ⏰ Daily 8–5

A boat tour of the large Laguna de Oviedo in Parque Nacional Jaragua provides a great opportunity for bird watching

Where to... Stay

Prices

Expect to pay per double room per night, excluding 22 per cent tax (10 per cent service charge, 12 per cent government tax)

$ under US$50 $$ US$50–100 $$$ over US$100

BAHORUCO

Barcelo Bahoruco $$

This is the only all-inclusive resort in the southwest and part of a chain that has properties all over the country. It is located in Bahoruco, about 16km (10 miles) south of Barahona along Highway 44, and while its facilities are not as varied as those at other all-inclusives on the north and east coasts, the rates are less expensive and they do include all meals and drinks. There is an attractive dining area and bar as well as a large pool. All rooms have cable TV and there are musicians in the bar in the evenings.

✠ 183 F5 ✉ Highway 44, Bahoruco ☎ 524 1111; fax: 524 6060; barcelobahoruco@codetel.net.do

Casa Bonita $–$$

Located on a small hill just beside Highway 44 in Bahoruco, this small resort has just a dozen cabins made of concrete and thatch, all with air-conditioning and hot water. There is a lovely swimming pool and an attractive bar as well as a dining room. Breakfast and dinner are included in the room rate. The atmosphere is very laid-back – at times it's difficult to find service.

✠ 183 F5 ✉ Calle Federico Geraldino 87, Bahoruco ☎ 445 8810

Coral Sol Resort $

This is another place that is tricky to find – look out for the small sign to the east of Highway 44 about 3km (2 miles) south of Bahoruco. Coral Sol styles itself as an **eco-resort** and is certainly very lush. There are just nine cabins with two bedrooms and bathrooms. There are two different rates here – one with breakfast included and the other with breakfast and dinner – and both are very reasonable.

✠ 183 F5 ✉ Off Highway 44, 3km (2 miles) south of Bahoruco ☎ 233 4882; www.coralsolresort.com

BARAHONA

Club Hotel Quemaito $–$$

Quemaito is the first good beach along Highway 44 south of Barahona, and this small hotel provides a relaxing spot to stay, though you'll have to look carefully for the sign directing you down a narrow lane off the main road. Of the dozen rooms here, eight have air-conditioning, four have fans and a few have sea views. The compound also has a small swimming pool and a large lawn. There are different rates for room only, half-board and full-board.

✠ 180 C1 ✉ Juan Esteban, Km10 Carreterra Barahona–Paraíso ☎ 223 0999; www.stodomingo.cjb.net

LAS SALINAS

Salinas Hotel $$

This small but smart hotel in the tiny village of Las Salinas makes an ideal base for exploring the nearby sand dunes and salt flats, as well as windsurfing and taking trips around the Bahía de las Calderas. This is a huge bay, of which the hotel has a panoramic view beyond its small swimming pool and solitary palm tree. There are 45 rooms and rates include all meals and drinks. There is also a diving school based here.

✠ 181 E1 ✉ Puerto Hermoso 7, Las Salinas ☎ 346 8855

Where to...
Eat and Drink

Prices
Expect to pay per person for a meal, excluding drinks, tips and tax (22 per cent)
$ under US$2   **$$** US$2–5   **$$$** over US$5

BARAHONA

Asadero Los Robles $–$$

If you're looking for somewhere lively to eat in Barahona, check out this place on the coastal road in the centre of town. With shaded benches in a garden area, it is very popular among locals, especially the young crowd, and gets very busy in the evenings. Grilled meat and seafood are the most popular dishes, and everything is reasonably priced. Loud *merengue* and *bachata* music gives the place an authentic Dominican atmosphere.

➕ 180 C1 ⊠ Avenida Enriquillo at the corner of Calle Nuestra Señora del Rosario ☎ 524 1629 ⏰ Mon–Fri 4 pm–late, Sat–Sun 10 am–late

Brisas del Caribe $$–$$$

Situated at the northern end of Avenida Enriquillo, which runs along the coast in Barahona, this smart, open-sided restaurant is well-named, as it usually enjoys a fresh breeze coming off the ocean. The waiters here are smartly dressed and the service is excellent. The extensive menu has many appealing seafood dishes such as prawns with garlic and grilled lobster, and there are plenty of drinks on offer too. Though it gets few foreign visitors as most of them stay in hotels far from town, it is very popular among well-to-do locals, and reservations for dinner are recommended.

➕ 180 C1 ⊠ Avenida Enriquillo, Barahona ☎ 524 2794 ⏰ Daily 9 am–11 pm

La Rocca $$–$$$

This is another open-sided restaurant on the coast road in Barahona, located about 5km (3 miles) south of the centre, though it does not have attractive sea views and gentle sea breezes like Brisas del Caribe. The menu covers a wide range of dishes, including beef and chicken and several alternatives prepared Chinese style. The speciality – as you might expect – is seafood, such as conch in garlic sauce, lobster thermidor, barbecued prawns and grilled barracuda. A good range of drinks including wine, beer and cocktails is also available and service is usually efficient and friendly.

➕ 180 C1 ⊠ Avenida Enriquillo 14 ☎ 970 7630 ⏰ Daily 9 am–10 pm

LAS SALINAS

Salinas $–$$

Even if you do not stay overnight at this cosy hotel in Las Salinas, it makes a convenient place to rest and eat while looking at the nearby sand dunes, salt flats and beach. The dining area consists of an open, breezy patio, with an idyllic view of the bay, and the friendly staff does its best to serve up a memorable meal. The house speciality is lobster, prepared Dominican-style, but the *lambi* (conch) is also very good, as are prawns cooked in garlic. The place is very popular with Dominicans and can get full at the weekends as it is within driving distance of Santo Domingo.

➕ 181 E1 ⊠ Puerto Hermoso 7, Las Salinas ☎ 346 8855 ⏰ Daily 8 am–11 pm

Where to... Shop

Since the southwest is the least developed region of the DR in terms of tourism, it follows that there are limited opportunities for souvenir shopping.

Virtually all visitors to the area pass through Santo Domingo, where there is the widest choice in the country, so it is best to plan your shopping there (▶ 63). However, the southwest is the only place in the world where larimar is mined, so prices for this beautiful stone are cheaper here.

BAHORUCO

There are no gift shops geared to tourists in the main towns of the southwest (Barahona, Baní and San Cristóbal), and the only place you will find a display of amber and larimar, Haitian paintings, rum and cigars is in the gift shop at the all-inclusive **Barceló Bahoruco Resort** (▶ 135). Also, if you spend much time on the southwest beaches, you will probably be approached by beach vendors selling small items of inexpensive jewellery from a portable case.

BARAHONA

The DR produces some of the best coffee in the world, and if you enjoy a cup yourself, you might like to take a look round the **Melo Coffee Factory** in Barahona at Calle Anacaona 10 (open Mon–Sat 8–5), where beans grown in the Cordillera Central are processed ready for export. To arrange an informal tour of the factory, ask the proprietor of Melo's Café next door. When passing along Highway 44 southwest of Barahona in the region of Arroyo, keep an eye open for locals selling **larimar** at the roadside. As the larimar mines (▶ 133)

are located nearby, prices can be very inexpensive, but most of the pieces on sale are rough and uncut, so it is difficult to gauge the quality. Nonetheless, larimar makes an ideal memento of the DR.

CABRAL

The small town of **Cabral**, just 15km (9 miles) northwest of Barahona, is famous for its **carnival masks** and if you ask at the park office of the Laguna Cabral (Cabral Lagoon just north of town, you may be able to buy one of these elaborate and colourful objects. They make striking wall hangings, though they are bulky and fragile, so rather awkward to transport back home. If you happen to be here during *Semana Santa* – Easter week, you can join the celebration of *Carnaval Cimarrón*, when everyone dresses up in bright outfits and dons devils' masks. Things also get pretty wild during the patron saint festival to La

LOS PATOS

Pula $–$$

The beaches to the southwest of Barahona, like Playa San Rafael and Los Patos, draw crowds of visitors who inevitably get hungry and thirsty during their stay. They are generally well-catered to by food and drink stalls on the beach, but if you would prefer to sit down in a restaurant to eat, head to this place on the main road in Los Patos opposite the church (Iglesia San Miguel). They serve excellent seafood here, prepared in either Italian or local *criollo* style. The pescado con coco (fish in coconut) is particularly delicious, as the chivo guisado, or goat stew, served with rice and beans. Wash it down with a refreshing ice-cold beer while watching the sea and listening to waves crashing on the beach in the background.

➕ 183 E5 ✉ Highway 44, Los Patos
🕓 Daily 10–10

Señora de los Remedios from 3–9 September.

The **local markets** of the region are always interesting to stroll around, and even if you don't find any neat souvenirs, you will probably find a few types of food that you have never seen before and also get a feel for natural Dominican friendliness. Of course, if you're planning to spend a day on the beach, it's a good idea to stock up on succulent fresh fruit for a picnic, and local markets are the best place to do this. Other picnic items on offer include bottled water, ice, a selection of suasages and cheeses and fresh bread.

If you happen to be passing through **Bani** during May–July, stop at one of the roadside stalls to sample the sweet and delicious **mangoes** for which the town is famous. Other purchases possible at small markets in this region include locally-grown coffee, cheap cigars for domestic consumption and *dulces criollos* or local sweets.

Where to...
Be Entertained

As with shopping, so it is with entertainment in the southwest. Most visitors to the region are attracted by its geographical diversity and natural appeal: they find plenty to keep themselves busy during the day and relax quietly in the evening. Though the beaches are the main attraction, the strong waves along most of the coast mean that there are few watersports on offer, and nightlife is limited to a few rough and ready nightclubs in Barahona.

WATERSPORTS

If you are a **windsurfing** or **diving** enthusiast, head for Las Salinas and contact the staff at the Salinas Hotel, who can arrange dive trips, tours of the bay and windsurfing. The tiny town sees few foreign visitors and has an authentic Dominican feel to it.

The most popular daytime entertainment for Dominican visitors to the southwest is relaxing by one of the many refreshing *balnearios*, or natural swimming pools in the region. Two of the most popular are at **Playa San Rafael** and **Los Patos** (▶ 131), because here it is easy to alternate between swimming in the sea and then cooling off in fresh water. There are also several *balnearios* around Lago Enriquillo, of which the one at **La Descubierta** is probably the most cool and refreshing (▶ 167). It's also a good place to rest up for a picnic.

NIGHTLIFE

At night most people are content to sit back at their hotel to recuperate and prepare for another busy day of exploration, swimming or just plain relaxation. However, if your feet get itchy for action, head into Barahona and check out the local nightclubs, where the music is all *merengue* and *bachata*. Two of the better local venues, **Lotus** and **Legends** are both located beside Parque Central, and get going around midnight. If you're more in the mood for a lively bar, **La Campina** is also next to the park, while the **Asadero Los Robles** (▶ 136) a popular hang-out for the local young crowd is down on the coast road near the centre of town. The music is distinctively Dominican and this is a good place to meet people and brush up on your Spanish.

If you are staying at **Barcelo Bahoruco** (▶ 135) the in-house entertainment includes live music and dancing in the evening.

Cibao Valley and Cordillera Central

Getting Your Bearings

Since the Dominican Republic is best known as a beach destination, few visitors explore its interior. However, nature enthusiasts and thrill seekers can turn this to their advantage, for the country's mountains and valleys contain some glorious scenery, and the rugged terrain lends itself well to adventure sports. It is also very easy and quick to drive into the interior, as the Autopista Duarte (Highway 1) connects Santo Domingo with Santiago de los Caballeros in the Cibao Valley near the north coast.

The Cibao Valley is sheltered by the mountain ranges of Cordillera Septentrional in the north and the Cordillera Central further south. It carries the country's principal river, the Yaque del Norte, from the central highlands to the sea at Monte Cristi, in the extreme northwest of the DR. All along the valley, crops like tobacco, rice, bananas and oranges flourish in the fertile soil, and are sold in the bustling markets of Santiago.

The main town in the highlands of the Cordillera Central is Jarabacoa, a small but friendly place which enjoys a fresh, almost Alpine climate at just over 500m (1,640 feet) above sea level. From Jarabacoa you can trek to waterfalls, take a ride on horseback or go white-water rafting, among many other options. The ultimate challenge here is the climb up Pico Duarte (► 170), which at 3,087m (10,125 feet) is the highest point in the entire Caribbean.

Right: Centro de Recreo, Santiago de los Caballeros
Previous page: Sugar cane farmer near Santiago de los Caballeros

★ Don't Miss

At Your Leisure

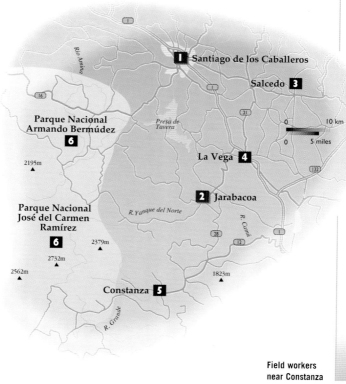

Río Amina

1 Santiago de los Caballeros

Salcedo 3

16

Presa de
Tavera

21

0 ———— 10 km

0 ———— 5 miles

**Parque Nacional
Armando Bermúdez
6**

2195m ▲

La Vega 4

132

2 Jarabacoa

R. Yanque del Norte

R. Camú

**Parque Nacional
José del Carmen
Ramírez
6**

2379m ▲

2732m ▲

28

12

2562m ▲

1823m ▲

Constanza 5

R. Grande

Field workers
near Constanza

Visit a folkloric museum and tobacco factory in Santiago, then head for the hills and waterfalls around Jarabacoa

Cibao Valley and Cordillera Central in Two Days

Day One

Morning

Start in the heart of ▮ **Santiago** (➤ 144) at Parque Duarte, which is flanked by the Catedral de Santiago Apostól and the Centro de Recreo, both of which are of architectural merit. From here go north a couple of blocks to the **Museo des Artes Folklórico Tomás Morel**, which is set within a colourful Victorian-style house.

Afternoon

If you're looking for souvenirs, drop by the **Mercado Modelo** (below) on Calle del Sol. Otherwise head straight for the city's most conspicuous building, the **Monumento a los Héroes de la Restauración de la República** (➤ 145). Complete the day with a tour of the Aurora Tabacalera (➤ 145), one of the biggest **cigar factories** in the country.

Evening

If your priority is to explore the nightlife, stay in Santiago and visit one of the city's many nightclubs (➤ 156). There's a galaxy of bars around Monumento a los Héroes de la Restauración de la República, of which Daiqui Loco (➤ 154) is recommended for snacks and daiquiris. You might also fancy a flutter at the casinos (➤ 156). Otherwise, move on to Jarabacoa where you will wake up to a much more scenic view the following day.

Day Two

Morning/Afternoon

If you spent the previous night in Santiago, head out early to 2 Jarabacoa (➤ 147) and make the most of the fresh mountain air. How you spend a day here depends on how adventurous you are. Most people arrive with a group to join a **white-water rafting** trip down the Río Yaque del Norte, which occupies most of a day. However, it can be equally rewarding to visit the town's two attractive waterfalls, **Salto de Jimenoa** and **Salto de Baiguate**, in the morning, then settle down for a picnic and lazy afternoon at the **Balneario La Confluencia**.

Evening

As with the daytime, there are both active and more tranquil alternatives for the evening. Either rest up at your hotel and relish the fresh, clean air and rural tranquility, or head for the Vista del Yaque (➤ 156) a few kilometres out of town and dance to one of the country's top *merengue* bands.

◘ Santiago de los Caballeros

Known by everyone simply as "Santiago", this is the Dominican Republic's second city, with a population approaching 1 million. It is an important centre for industry and agriculture, and the surrounding region of the Cibao Valley is often referred to as the nation's bread basket. Though not as dense with historical buildings as Santo Domingo, Santiago has plenty to keep you busy for a day or longer, including striking edifices, bustling markets and tobacco factories.

The "caballeros" (gentlemen) of the city's name refers to the group of 30 men who founded it in 1495, a few kilometres northeast of its current location. A devastating **earthquake** in 1562 totally destroyed the town, and it was rebuilt in its current location on the east bank of the Río Yaque del Norte. In the mid-17th century, when **tobacco** first became popular in Europe, Santiago was one of the first centres to export it, and remains a major producer today. The city has managed to retain its importance mostly because of convenient connections with both Santo Domingo to the south and Puerto Plata to the north.

Parque Duarte is a large shady square in the town centre with some of the city's most important buildings around it. Most prominent is the **Catedral de Santiago Apostól**, built in the late 19th century, but recently renovated. Its cavernous interior contains some interesting modern stained-glass windows and detailed carvings around the doorways. Also facing the square is the **Centro de Recreo**, built in the same period, though its distinctive Moorish influence contrasts

sharply with the Victorian style evident in most other build-ings around. The building is used as a private club, while the square itself serves as an informal meeting place where it is easy to strike up conversations. On the north side of the square you may see horse drawn carriages that offer rides around the city's sights.

A couple of blocks north of Parque Duarte, the **Museo des Artes Folklórico Tomás Morel** is housed in a brightly-painted but small Victorian house and is well worth visiting for its quirky collection of Dominicana. Apart from a clever cooling cupboard that passes as the DR's first fridge, there are carnival masks, *merengue* memorabilia and the paraphernalia of mixed Afro-Christian religions (► 13).

Santiago's most unmissable sight, visible from all over town, is the 67m-high (220 feet) **Monumento a los Héroes de la Restauración de la República**, sad-dled with a name almost as long as the building is tall. You'd win no prizes for guessing that the man behind this grandiose structure was Rafael Trujillo (► 10), who planned it to be a lasting memorial to himself. This dedication was revised after his death, and the monument now honours those Dominicans who lost their lives in gaining independence from the Spanish. If you are feeling energetic, you can clamber up the stairs inside for a fantastic view across the city.

Since Santiago is famous for tobacco production, it is worth taking a look at the process involved in making cigars, for which the DR, like Cuba is world renowned (► 18). At the **Aurora Tabacalera**, a huge cigar factory in the east of town, you can watch how the leaves are pressed and rolled into both small and big cigars. Before leaving the factory you will be offered a free glass of Presidente beer, and, of course, be

**Above:
Horse-drawn
carriage, a
great way to
see the city**

**Left:
Monumento a
los Héroes de
la Restauración
de la República**

encouraged to purchase a souvenir of your visit in the cigar gift shop.

TAKING A BREAK

In a city of this size there are plenty of alternatives, but a reliable choice is the **Pez Dorado** on Calle del Sol.

The rooftops of Santiago

✚ 181 E4

Museo des Artes Folklórico Tomás Morel
✉ Restauración 174
☎ 582 6787
🕐 Mon–Fri 9–1, 3–6
💵 Free

Aurora Tabacalera
✉ Jimenes 2 and Villa Progresa
☎ Tel: 241 1111
🕐 Mon–Sat 9:30–5
💵 Free

SANTIAGO DE LOS CABALLEROS: INSIDE INFO

Top tips Santiago's street system can be confusing for newcomers, so it makes sense to hire a motorbike, taxi or horse and carriage to take you around town. Don't forget to **agree a fee before starting**, or you may get taken for a ride in more ways than one.

Must see The **Museo des Artes Folklórico Tomás Morel** is a veritable goldmine of "Dominicana" crammed into a tiny space, and there is often an enthusiastic guide to show you around, although he doesn't speak much English.

2 Jarabacoa

This town of around 10,000 inhabitants enjoys some of the country's best weather and has long been a cool retreat for wealthy Dominicans. These days it also appears on the itineraries of tourists from beach resorts, who zip up into the hills for a day's white-water rafting or canyoning. However, it is worth savouring its scenic attractions slowly, and with so many adventure sports on offer, as well as comfortable accommodation, Jarabacoa makes an ideal destination for independent travellers.

Jarabacoa lies on the east bank of the Río Yaque del Norte (North Yaque River) and the fields and orchards around town are planted with fruits more common in temperate climates, like strawberries, raspberries and apples. Also on the surrounding hillsides are coffee plantations. Though the tiny town centre is pleasant enough and has most services you might require such as banks, convenience stores and internet cafés, the attractions of the region lie out of the centre.

Salto de Jimenoa

There are several **waterfalls** in the region, of which the two most popular to visit are Salto de Baiguate and Salto de Jimenoa. Both are located a few kilometres from the centre of town, and can be reached by car, motorbike or on horseback. The **Salto de Baiguate** is a little more difficult to access, gets less visitors and has a less impressive flow of water falling into a shallow pool below it. However, it is more peaceful, and the steep, thickly wooded slopes around make for appealing views. The short path that you need to walk along to get there from the parking area is often thick with butterflies.

The **Salto de Jimenoa** is about 40m (130 feet) high, and is easier to reach and carries a much greater volume of water, so receives many more visitors. From the parking area beside a military barracks, you need to walk over rocks and along swaying wooden walkways that border and then cross the river in order to get a view of the falls. The water thunders over a narrow gap in a rockface into a deep green pool below that makes a good place for a cooling dip. There is also a shaded refreshment stall that sells cold drinks right beside the fall.

Another, even higher waterfall, called **Salto de Jimenoa Uno**, is located further upstream on the Río Jimenoa, about 7km (4.5 miles) south of town off the road to Constanza. With a drop of over 60m (197 feet), this is the most spectacular fall in the region, but it is rather difficult to find, so it's best to take a guide if you want to see it.

In the northern suburbs of town, the **Balneario La Confluencia** is a popular spot for relaxation under trees by the confluence of the Yaque del Norte and Jimenoa rivers. The water is quite shallow here and the current not very strong near the banks, so it is a popular spot for swimming, or at least splashing about. Horse owners roam the area, offering **horseback** rides along the riverbanks, and at the weekends big groups of Dominicans arrive loaded up with baskets of goodies as well as the inevitable *merengue* boom box.

What attracts most foreigners to Jarabacoa, however, is not waterfalls and picnics but the adrenalin rush that accompanies the many adventure sports on offer. Top of the list in popularity is **white-water rafting** through the rapids of the Río Yaque del Norte, an exciting but not particularly dangerous experience that costs around US$60 per head for a day's outing. Rafters are taken along the road towards La Ciénaga to the southwest of town, where they are given a helmet, a lifejacket and a safety lesson. They are then assigned to an inflated rubber raft with a group of half a dozen others, one of whom is the guide and captain of the raft.

Once the raft is in the water, the paddlers' job is to steer it between the boulders that protrude from the river like an obstacle course. Needless to say, with a few

A footbridge near Salto de Jimenoa

novices aboard, it is not unusual for the rafts to get stuck on the rocks or spin round and glide backwards downstream, but such mishaps are all just part of the fun. If you've never tried white-water rafting before, this is a good place to give it a go, though if you're an experienced rafter, you might consider it an insufficient challenge as there are no really difficult rapids to run.

There are plenty of other adventure sports on offer, such as **canyoning**, which involves trekking, leaping, swimming and rappelling down cliff faces along a stretch of the Río Jimenoa. For something a little less demanding, sign up for a jeep safari, or a quad or mountain bike tour. If you're looking for an even greater challenge and have a few days to spare, sign up for a trek to **Pico Duarte** (➤ panel, page 170).

White-water rafting on the Río Yaque del Norte

TAKING A BREAK

If you sign up for a tour then lunch will be included, but if you're looking for somewhere in town with a varied menu and reliable food, check out **El Rancho** (➤ 154), located on Avenida Independencia.

➕ 181 E3
✉ 155km (97 miles) northwest of Santo Domingo
🚌 *Guagua* from La Vega every 30 mins

JARABACOA: INSIDE INFO

Top tips The waterfalls and the Balneario La Confluencia can get **crowded** with Dominicans **at weekends**, so if you're looking for a rural idyll, time your visit for midweek.

• For a bumpy but enjoyable drive that offers **great views** from mountain ridges, take the rough road to Constanza (➤ 151), about 50km (30 miles) to the south. This is best done in a 4WD vehicle, especially after rain.

In more detail For more **information about adventure sports** on offer around Jarabacoa, check out the following websites:
www.ranchobaiguate.com.do
www.hispaniola.com/whitewater

At Your Leisure

Smiling farmers near Constanza

3 Salcedo

Located about 30km (19 miles) east of Santiago in a region of coffee and cacao plantations, Salcedo is a small town that illustrates a grisly episode in the country's history. At the entrance to the town are portraits on a wall of the three Mirabal sisters, who proved such a thorn in the side of General Trujillo (➤ 10) that he arranged for them to be assassinated in November 1960. In the Plazoleta de las Hermanas Mirabal, a few kilometres east of Salcedo, is the frame of the car in which they died and a sculpture to their memory. Also nearby is the Museo de las Hermanas Mirabal, which contains photographs and personal effects of these three Dominican heroines.

➕ 181 F4 ✉ Highway 132 east of Santiago

4 La Vega

This is a busy industrial city on the Autopista Duarte (Highway 1) southeast of Santiago that suddenly bursts into life at **carnival time** (February).

Its buildings are drab and boring, and even the concrete cathedral built in 1992 beside the central square in town is considered one of the ugliest structures in the country – a misconceived hotchpotch of modern and colonial design elements. However, if you happen to be here on a Sunday in February, you can witness some wild scenes as everyone dresses up in carnival masks and bright clothes to create havoc on the streets. This is purported to be the liveliest carnival celebration in the country, but watch out for a pig's bladder full of water to surprisingly drench you.

➕ 181 E3 ✉ Highway 1, southeast of Santiago

5 Constanza

Situated in a valley at an altitude of 1,300m (4,264 feet), Constanza is a small town with little of interest in itself, though the surrounding fields of strawberries, garlic and roses make for picturesque views. At this

altitude, the temperature gets downright cold in the winter months, a tremendous novelty for tropical dwellers, and there are several mansions of rich Dominicans tucked away on the valley's edge. Back in the 1950s, General Trujillo brought many Japanese families here to introduce their methods of agriculture, and they have since settled and intermarried into the community. Despite the hills around being deforested, there are some good hiking trails in the region. The Cabañas de la Montaña hotel, located to the east of town, can point you in the right direction or arrange for a guide to accompany you.

➕ 181 D2 ✉ About 50km (30 miles) south of Jarabacoa

❻ Parques Nacionales Armando Bermúdez and José del Carmen Ramírez

These two national parks which border each other in the Central Cordillera cover an area of over 1,500sq km (585sq miles). They contain the highest mountains in the

Washing clothes in the Río Yaque del Norte, near Pico Duarte

Caribbean, including the biggest of them all, **Pico Duarte**, at 3,087m (10,125 feet) which makes a challenging trek of several days (➤ panel, page 170). This part of the country is so rugged that it is difficult for humans to access, meaning that there is a wealth of wildlife including wild boar, and birds such as parrots and woodpeckers within the parks' boundaries. You will need to be accompanied by a guide on any trek that you make, and there are cabins where you can stay, but facilities of course are basic.

Parque Nacional Armando Bermúdez and Parque Nacional José del Carmen Ramírez
➕ 181 D3 ⏰ Daily 6 am–5 pm
🏛 There are several ranger stations at various entrances to the national parks.
💲 Expensive

Where to... Stay

Prices

Expect to pay per double room per night, excluding 22 per cent tax (10 per cent service charge, 12 per cent government tax)

$ under US$50 $$ US$50–100 $$$ over US$100

JARABACOA

Gran Jimenoa $–$$

Located beside the river just a couple of kilometres from the centre of Jarabacoa, this relatively new three-storey hotel gives excellent value for money. The rooms are very spacious, all have air-conditioning and TVs, and breakfast is included in the price. There is also a pool and hot tub on the premises.

➕ 181 E3 ☒ Avenida La Confluencia, Los Corralitos, Jarabacoa ☎ 574 6304

Pinar Dorado $–$$

This attractive building, looking something like an alpine lodge, makes a great base in Jarabacoa. Run by the owners of Rancho Baiguate, it is situated a little east of the centre of town on the road to Constanza. All of its 40 or so rooms are comfortably equipped with air-conditioning, cable TV and hot-water bathrooms, and many have lovely views of the swimming pool surrounded by pine trees. There is an attractive restaurant and reasonably-priced meal plans are available. The staff are also very helpful.

➕ 181 E3 ☒ Carretera Jarabacoa – Constanza Km 1, Jarabacoa ☎ 574 2820; fax: 574 2231; pinardorado@codetel.net.do

Rancho Baiguate $–$$

This rambling ranch covering a huge area to the east of Jarabacoa is one of the country's best-known adventure sports centres, so its 17 rooms are very popular with people who want to participate in some of the activities on offer locally, like white-water rafting, canyoning, horse riding and quad safaris (▶ 148). The rooms set in cabins scattered around the site don't have air-conditioning, but they do have hot water, fans and mosquito screens. There is also a swimming pool, football pitch, basketball court and fishing pond. Buffet meals are included in the price.

➕ 181 E3 ☒ Carretera Jarabacoa–Constanza Km 5, Jarabacoa ☎ 574 6890; fax: 574 4940; www.ranchobaiguate.com

SANTIAGO DE LOS CABALLEROS

Colonial $

This hotel conveniently located near the centre of Santiago is ideal if you need to watch your pesos. From the front it looks small but in fact has 60 rooms split between a new and an old building. There is a variety of rooms, some rather small and cramped and others large, some with fans and some with air-conditioning, at a range of prices. They have no frills or fancy décor but are kept clean, and represent excellent value at very low rates.

➕ 181 E4 ☒ Calle Salvador Cucurullo 113–115, Santiago ☎ 247 3122; fax: 582 0811; hotelcolonial@codetel.net.do

Gran Almirante $$$

Set in a well-to-do suburb a couple of kilometres northeast of the centre of Santiago, this elegant hotel is a good option if you can afford it. It has three restaurants, a casino, tennis courts, a fitness centre, a business centre, a pool and a lively nightclub among its amenities. Its 156 rooms are luxuriously decorated and all are equipped with air-conditioning, hot-water bathrooms,

Where to...
Eat and Drink

mini-bar and cable TV.

181 E4 ☒ **Avenida Estrella Sadhalá, Santiago** ☎ **580 1992; fax: 241 1492; www.hodelpa.com**

Matún $$

Smaller, less expensive and more centrally located in Santiago than the Gran Almirante, this hotel is next to the towering Monumento a los Héroes de la Restauración de la República. Originally built during the Trujillo era, it has recently been renovated, and its 50 rooms are well-maintained and all have cable TV. Facilities include a pool, a nightclub and a casino. This is a particularly good location if you want to check out Santiago's nightlife, as there are several bars and clubs within easy walking distance. If you don't feel like going out, there's a good restaurant serving a variety of *criollo* and international dishes, as well as a well-stocked bar.

181 E4 ☒ **Avenida Las Carreras, Santiago** ☎ **581 3107; fax: 581 8415**

Prices

Expect to pay per person for a meal, excluding drinks, tips and tax (22 per cent)

$ under US$2   **$$** US$2–5   **$$$** over US$5

CONSTANZA

Lorenzo's $–$$

If you make the worthwhile trip to Constanza (▲ 151), you might well want to stop there for a bite to eat, and the best all-round choice here is Lorenzo's. There's nothing special about the ambience, with the TV usually jabbering away to itself, but the place is clean, the staff welcoming, and the menu is wide ranging, with Dominican and international dishes. Choose from sandwiches, pastas, steaks and Dominican specialities like *mofongo* (▲ 24). There are even a few exotic dishes like *guinea al vino* (guinea fowl in wine) and *conejo al vino* (rabbit in wine).

181 D2 ☒ **Calle Luperón 83, Constanza** ☎ **539 2008** ☺ **Daily 7 am–11 pm**

JARABACOA

El Rancho $$–$$$

Located just north of the centre of Jarabacoa, this excellent restaurant is run by the owners of Rancho Baiguate, who clearly have a good idea of what appeals to foreign visitors. The place is open-sided and the interior walls display striking art by Dominican artists, some of whom live locally. There's plenty of choice here, including pizzas and pastas, plus a tempting range of seafood, chicken and beef dishes, and prices are reasonable for the quality. The relaxed ambience might encourage you to indulge in a bottle of wine from the wide selection, and you can finish the meal off with a cappuccino or espresso coffee.

181 E3 ☒ **Corner of Avenidas Independencia & Norberto Tiburcio** ☺ **Tue–Sun breakfast, lunch and dinner**

SANTIAGO DE LOS CABALLEROS

Daiqui Loco $

This outdoor bar is a great place to sit back and watch the inhabitants of Santiago going about their business while you enjoy a snack and a drink. The grilled sandwiches, hamburgers, burritos, French fries and other snacks here are all excellent and reasonably priced, while frozen daiquiris are the house speciality. Go easy on these, as they are stronger than they seem.

➕ 181 E4 ✉ Avenida Juan Pablo Duarte, Santiago ⏰ Daily noon–late

Pez Dorado $$–$$$

Conveniently situated near the centre of Santiago, this fancy restaurant serves top-quality Dominican food as well as some very passable Chinese dishes including sweet-and-sour and stir-fried rice. There are lots of intriguing seafood dishes made with prawns, fish, squid and octopus, as well as chicken prepared in various tasty sauces. The wine list is fairly extensive, including both local and imported vintages, and – as usual in better DR restaurants – there's a good selection of rum-based cocktails. The restful ambience and attentive service make this a good spot to rest up after the rigours of sightseeing.

➕ 181 E4 ✉ Calle del Sol 43, Santiago ☎ 582 2518 ⏰ Daily noon–midnight

BONAO

Típico Bonao $$–$$$

If you fancy a meal break while driving between Santo Domingo and Santiago on the Autopista Duarte (Highway 1), pull into one of these two cleverly located roadside restaurants just north of Bonao. The first, at Km83 from Santo Domingo, is accessible to traffic going north or south, while the second at Km90 from Santo Domingo can be reached only by northbound vehicles. The décor is very smart, the service polite and efficient, and the menu, which includes Dominican and international dishes, brings in a constant stream of the road-weary. Whether you need a full meal and relaxation afterwards or if you just want a break to stretch your legs and get a shot of caffeine, this is an excellent choice. They serve a good, strong locally-grown coffee too.

➕ 181 F3 ✉ Autopista Duarte, Km83 & Km90 ☎ 248 7924 ⏰ Daily early–late

Where to...
Shop

Despite being a big city, Santiago doesn't offer many shopping opportunities. For amber and larimar jewellery, or Haitian and Dominican paintings, you are better off looking in Santo Domingo or Puerto Plata. However, it does have a Mercado Modelo selling inexpensive souvenirs, and as the heart of the tobacco industry in the DR, Santiago is also the place to buy the best cigars at the factory outlets. In the tiny town of Jarabacoa, choices are limited, though a walk round the local markets for an interesting experience and the possibility of finding a rewarding or unusual purchase.

There are plenty of shops in Santiago, but virtually all of them are stocked with local necessities that are unlikely to be of interest to visitors from afar. One place that does sell a range of inexpensive souvenirs like conch shells, straw hats and T-shirts is the **Mercado Modelo**, located just over a block east of Parque Duarte on the south side of Calle del Sol. Since it is so near the main sights in the city centre, it is worth checking out.

Santiago is the best place in the country to shop for **cigars**, as the major factories are located here. Two of them are open to the public for tours and, of course, provide visitors with the chance to buy a box to take home. In the town centre, **La Habana Tabacalera** at the corner of Calle 16 de Agosto and Calle San Luis (Mon–Fri 8:30–4:30; admission free) is the longest-established tobacco company in the country.

Where to...
Be Entertained

As the country's second city and the traditional home of *bachata* music, Santiago has a vibrant nightlife. Things are more laid back in the hills of Jarabacoa, but the Vista del Yaque nightclub a few kilometres out of town draws big crowds. There are enough sights to see in Santiago and plenty of adventure sports in Jarabacoa to keep most people busy during the day.

ADVENTURE SPORTS AND GOLF

Many people make long day trips to **Jarabacoa** from the all-inclusive resorts on the north coast and other parts of the country just to partici-

pate in one of the **adventure sports** on offer (▶ 148). There is also a decent nine-hole **golf course** open to the public, which is located north of town on the road to Salto de Jimenoa (▶ 147)

NIGHTLIFE

Santiago has plenty of bars and clubs. Many of the city's liveliest **bars** are concentrated around the Monumento a los Héroes de la Restauración de la República, of which **Bar Code**, at Calle Cuba 25, and **Talanca**, at the corner of Calles Restauración and Tolentino, are worth checking out. For a good **nightclub**, head for **Alcázar** in the centrally located Gran Almirante Hotel or **Ambis I** and **Ambis II** on

the Autopista Duarte about 2km (1.25 miles) out of town. There are **casinos** in the Gran Almirante and Matúm Hotels, and a **multi-screen cinema**, Hollywood 7, at the corner of Calles Estrella Sadhalá and Argentina.

Considering that **Jarabacoa** is such a small town, it has quite an active nightlife. If you happen to be here during the baseball season (Nov–Feb), it's worth checking out the **baseball games** most evenings at the field on Calle La Confluencia, not only for the action on the pitch, but also for the lively antics of the enthusiastic crowd.

There are also a few small nightclubs in the centre of Jarabacoa, of which **Plaza Central**, at the junction of Calles Sánchez and Colón near Parque Central, and **Antillas**, at the junction of Avenidas Independencia and Norberto Tiburcio, are probably the best. The most popular night spot is actually a few kilometres southwest of town – the **Vista del Yaque**, which draws

big crowds who dance to the driving beat of live bands. Access is via a wobbly footbridge over the Río Yaque del Norte, so take care on arriving and leaving, especially if you have had a few drinks.

FESTIVALS

As a city of almost a million music and dance lovers, **Santiago** is one of the best places to be during **Carnival**, when local residents deck themselves out in wild outfits and congregate around the monument to sing, dance and create general mayhem. Sundays in February are the time to be there, and the climax of festivities comes on 27 February, when a parade and musicians take to the streets to celebrate **Independence Day** in considerable style. Another date to remember is 22 July, when the *fiesta patronale* or **patron saint festival** for Santiago Apostal gives everyone the opportunity for drinking and dancing in the streets again.

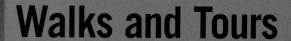
Walks and Tours

1 ZONA COLONIAL SANTO DOMINGO

Walk

DISTANCE 1.5km (1 mile)
TIME 2 hours
START/END POINT Parque Colón
⊞ 185 E4

Fine locally designed ceramics on show in the Zona Colonial

PLAZA ESPAÑA

GENERAL CABRAL

EMILIANO TEJERA

ISABEL LA CATÓLICA

6 Casa de la Moneda

MERCEDES

LAS

5 Monasterio de San Francisco

4 Hospital de San Nicolás de Bari

GENERAL LUPERON

DUARTE

MACORIS

0 200 metres
0 200 yards

Metal carvings of some highly individual and expressive heads on the western gates of Catedral de Santa María la Menor

boutiques selling clothing and jewellery.

Opposite the plaza, on the south side of Calle Padre Billini, is **Casa Tostado**, a renovated 16th-century building built with a combination of Gothic and Moorish architecture. It is named after Francisco Tostado,

Taking a Break

Although this is not such a taxing walk, you might want to rest your legs for a while in the peaceful courtyard of the **Museo de la Familia Dominicana**. Alternatively, there are benches just further on at Plaza Duarte which enjoy shade from the fierce rays of the sun.

Museo de la Familia Dominicana
☒ Casa Tostado, corner of Padre Billini and Arzobispo Meriño ◎ Mon–Sat 9–4
◍ Inexpensive

This short walk around Santo Domingo's colonial quarter gives a good sense of the city's great age, as well as the strong spirit in the residents of today. After passing the New World's first university and hospital, as well as the shell of an early Franciscan monastery, it winds back to the centre of town via some appealing shops.

1–2

Start the tour in Parque Colón, where shady pipal trees stand in each corner and conversation buzzes in the cafés that spill on to the square. Leave the square by the **southwest corner**, walking south on **Calle Arzobispo Meriño**. Take a moment to admire the expressive faces carved on the west gate of the Catedral de Santa María la Menor. This view of the cathedral and unshaded bell tower is

very photogenic and particularly attractive in the afternoon light. Continue walking south, passing Arzobispo Nouel, to the end of the next block, where there is a small square on the left, **Plaza Padre Billini**. This square commemorates a 17th-century priest who fought for the rights of the poor. Ironically, these days the plaza is bordered by expensive

Parque Colón

Catedral de Santa María la Menor

①

Plaza Padre Billini

② Casa Tostado

ARZOBISPO MERIÑO

SALOME UREÑA

EL CONDE

19 DE MARZO

ARZOBISPO NOUEL

Parque Duarte

Plaza Fray Bartolomé de las Casas

PADRE BILLINI

HOSTOS

③

Convento de los Dominicos

the first university professor to be born in the colony. The house contains the seldom-visited **Museo de la Familia Dominicana** which is furnished in the style of a well-to-do Dominican family of the 19th century.

2–3

From here, go west along **Calle Padre Billini** for one block, passing Plaza Fray Bartolomé de las Casas on the left, where a statue of a monk who petitioned the Spanish Crown on behalf of the Taíno Indians raises a fist from the folds of his robes. At the end of this block, there is a shady square (Plaza Duarte) to the right and the **Convento de los Dominicos** (▲ 56), which was the first university to be established in the Americas, to the left (entrance on Avenida Duarte). The convent is open for services in the morning and evening, and the walls and vault of the Chapel of the Rosary (just on the right inside the entrance) are covered with vibrant murals.

3–4

Turn right from Calle Padre Billini on to **Calle Hostos** at Parque Duarte and walk north on this street for two blocks. Cross Calle El Conde and walk on up Hostos one and a half blocks. On your right are the ruins of the **Hospital de San Nicolás de Bari** (▲ 56), the first hospital in the Americas.

4–5

Keep walking north on **Calle Hostos**. After it crosses Calle Las Mercedes, it goes up a slight rise, and above the road on the left is an attractive crescent of colourful wooden houses. At the top of the slope the road

Parque Colón's numerous cafés are a good place to sit and relax

bends to the right and here on the left are yet more 16th-century ruins, this time of the **Monasterio de San Francisco**. When built in 1544, it was intended to represent Spain's great religious strength, but down the years it took a battering from the pirate fleets under the command of British privateer, Sir Francis Drake (▲ 16) as well as from frequent earthquakes. All that remain today are foundations and a few walls, yet the hush that prevails creates a strong sense of the past.

5–6

Go back to Calle Hostos and branch on to **Calle Emiliano Tejera**. Walk down the short slope to the next junction at Calle Arzobispo Meriño, then turn right on to this major shopping street. As you walk south, look out on your right for a striking frieze of faces, thought to represent the five ages of man, above the entrance to number 358, the **Casa de la Moneda**. After this, you are likely to be distracted by bright displays of Haitian and Dominican art, as well as the extensive range of other knicknacks, trinkets and local souvenirs, until you find yourself back in **Parque Colón**, right beside the El Conde Restaurant, which has very good food and all manner of drinks at reasonable prices.

Piles of coconut husks in a clearing just west of Las Terrenas

2 SAMANÁ PENINSULA
Drive & Horse Trek

DISTANCE 85km (53 miles)
TIME 6–7 hours (including 3-hour trek)
START/END POINT Las Terrenas
🖪 182 C4

The Samaná Peninsula is packed with fantastic landscapes, both on the coast and up in the hills. This drive gives a good taste of the rugged countryside with constantly changing views, and a horseback trek to a beautiful waterfall in the jungle adds a touch of adventure to the outing.

1–2

Leave **Las Terrenas** (▶ 88) heading east along the road to El Portillo. To your left, gentle waves break on golden beaches overhung by palm trees. After a few kilometres the road bends inland away from the coast and passes the tiny airport of El Portillo, which is nothing more than a field with a landing strip, opposite the El Portillo Beach Resort, one of the few all-inclusives on the peninsula. The road then begins to climb into the hills, passing the village of La Barbacoa, and with lush vegetation crowding both sides between

villages. When you reach **El Limón**, you will see several places advertising **horseback rides to Salto El Limón** (El Limón Waterfall). Make an agreement with one of these outfits if you didn't already book in Las Terrenas (see below). Then park the car and get ready for some fun.

2–3

Most operators offer the horseback ride to the falls, which takes 2–3 hours, and a meal afterwards, for around US$10. This is excellent value, but doesn't include any payment for your guide: US$2 is a standard tip. The guide leads the horse while you ride in comfort, identifying common tropical fruits such as pineapples, mangoes and bananas along the way. The route crosses shallow rivers and climbs along narrow jungle tracks (very slippery after rain) to a high vantage point, with views down over the north coast, then continues to a tethering point

its base is just too much to resist after that tiring walk down. When you've had a refreshing dip and taken a few photos, scramble back up the hill, mount the horse and mosey on down to El Limón for lunch. Then continue in the same direction along the road from Las Terrenas to **Samaná**, which is about 20km (12 miles) away over a ridge of hills.

3–4

Officially known as **Santa Bárbara de Samaná**, this small port has always attracted sailors for its protected anchorage and its fine views over Bahía de Samaná (Samaná Bay). These days it is a bustling point of embarkation for **whale-watching trips** around the bay (▶ 90) as well as day trips to the island of **Cayo Levantado**. This drive provides a good opportunity to stretch your legs by wandering round the market, La Churcha and the Nature Centre.

When you're set to move on, take Highway 5 heading west out of town. This vital road stretches all the way from the Cibao Valley near Santiago, curling its way along the north coast, to **Las Galeras** (▶ 96) at the northeastern tip of the Samaná Peninsula. It is generally quite busy, and though the road seems to run beside the bay, it presents only a few

glimpses across the water before arriving at **Sánchez**.

4–5

The fishing port of Sánchez is the starting point for most trips to **Parque Nacional Los Haitises** (▶ 95), but there is little else of interest here, so look out for a turning to the right to Las Terrenas a few kilometres before reaching the town. Now begins the most exciting part of the drive, as this narrow country lane switchbacks its way up and over a ridge which is about 400m (1,312 feet) high, passing through colourful villages along the way. Take care on this road as it can be badly potholed after rain. Keep an eye open as the road climbs, and you will find a few spots where you can pull up to enjoy a magnificent

Horse Trekking in Las Terrenas

You might want to ensure availability by booking your horse trekking tour to Salto de Limón in advance before you leave Las Terrenas. If you book in El Limón, Casa Santi, just south of the main crossroads, is a good recommendation. Tel: 240 6261

Refreshing tranquillity at Salto El Limón

for the horses beside a small shack selling refreshments. From here there is a fantastic view down over the waterfall, but it is even better from down below. This path is too steep for horses, so it's a tricky 15-minute clamber to get down to the inviting pool below the falls.

The towering 50-m high (164 feet) waterfall tumbles down a moss-covered cliff face in a network of ribbons, and the milky pool at

panorama of Bahía de Samaná and the Parque Nacional Los Haïtises – an enormous expanse of green and blue. After crossing the ridge, there are also a few places to stop on the way down to Las Terrenas with views of the north coast of the peninsula and three whale-shaped islands off the coast, suitably called Las Ballenas (the whales).

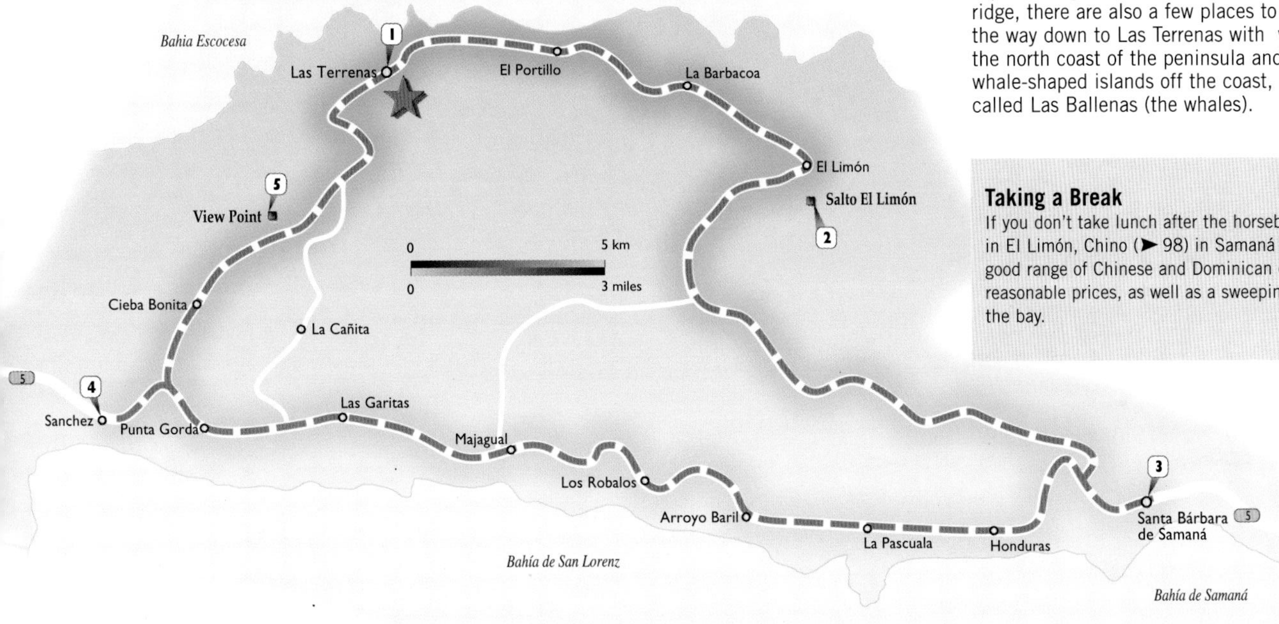

Taking a Break

If you don't take lunch after the horseback trek in El Limón, Chino (▶ 98) in Samaná offers a good range of Chinese and Dominican dishes at reasonable prices, as well as a sweeping view of the bay.

Bahía Escocesa

1 Las Terrenas

El Portillo

La Barbacoa

El Limón

2 Salto El Limón

5 View Point

Cieba Bonita

La Cañita

Las Garitas

Punta Gorda

4 Sanchez

Majagual

Los Robalos

Arroyo Baril

Bahía de San Lorenz

La Pascuala

Honduras

3 Santa Bárbara de Samaná

Bahía de Samaná

0   5 km
0   3 miles

3 THE LAGO ENRIQUILLO LOOP

Drive

DISTANCE 200km (138 miles)
TIME 8 hours
START/END POINT Barahona
🔖 181 C1

This drive around the largest saltwater lake in the Caribbean passes through some classic desert terrain, with cacti lining long stretches of roadside. You can feed tame iguanas on the shores of the lake, and watch crocodiles and flamingos on Isla Cabritos (▶ 134) in the centre of the lake. To cool down, take a dip in a refreshing mineral pool and then peek into neighbouring Haiti at the border town of Jimani.

Before You Go

Note that if you plan to visit the island of **Isla Cabritos**, you either need to leave Barahona very early in the morning, or stay in basic but clean accommodation in nearby La Descubierta, as boats like to make the trip in the morning.

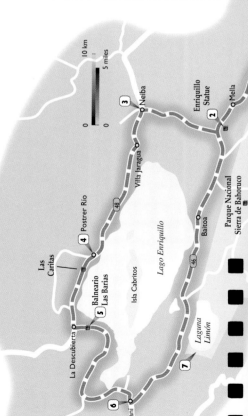

People waiting on the rickety jetty near La Descubierta for boats to Isla Cabritos

1-2

Leave **Barahona** heading northwest on Highway 44 and take the first major fork to the left a few kilometres out of town, on to Highway 46 heading towards **Cabral**. Once you get away from the coast the terrain is very inhospitable to humans – nothing but dry, caked earth and thorny bushes. The area is thinly populated, but the few villages that line the road bring diversion in the form of the colourful houses: the primrose and lime; claret and navy blue; rose and peach frontages show their occupants' great flair for design. After passing Cabral, you may catch a glimpse of the **Laguna del Rincón** to your right.

About 60km (37 miles) out of Barahona, the road arrives at a junction with a large **statue** of the *cacique* or Indian chief Enriquillo, after whom the nearby lake is named, set on a plinth in the middle of the road.

2-3

Turn right at the Enriquillo statue off of Highway 46 and head due north to **Neiba**. Though the lake is near, it remains out of

A Taíno Hero

With few exceptions, encounters between the Spanish and the peace-loving local population of Taínos were a simple matter of genocide, resulting in the extinction of these indigenous people during the first part of the 16th century. However, Enriquillo refused to work as a slave for the Spanish and organised his followers into a highly efficient guerrilla force, hiding in the mountains of the Sierra de Bahoruco to the south of the lake and the Sierra de Nieba to the north. In the 1530s, the Spanish gave up their efforts to capture him and signed a peace treaty allowing Enriquillo and his supporters to settle in the area.

A novel entitled *Enriquillo*, written by Manuel Jesús de Galván in the late 19th century, idealised the Indian chief's exploits and elevated him to the status of national hero. These days most Dominicans are proud of their Taíno heritage, yet little is known about their culture as Spanish efforts to exterminate them were so successful.

A heavily laden tree especially adapted to life at the edge of the salty Lago Enriquillo

sight to the west of the road. Neiba itself is a small town that has a reputation for growing grapes, and there is a busy market on Wednesdays and Saturdays.

3–4

At Neiba turn left on to **Highway 48**, also called the Carretera Enriquillo, and head due west. The first views of the lake are on the left soon after passing **Villa Jaragua**, and if the weather is clear there is also a good view of the mountains of the Sierra de Bahoruco to the south of the lake. The lake itself is over 200sq km (78sq miles), its waters are three times as salty as sea water, and it lies at about 40m (130 feet) below sea level – the lowest point in the Caribbean. The road is lined for much of the way by straggling cacti, and passes through small villages. At times the road climbs slightly, giving more views over the lake on the way to the town of **Postrer Río**.

4–5

A few kilometres beyond Postrer Río on the right are **Las Caritas**, some of the most famous **Taíno petroglyphs** in the country, carved into the coral rock overlooking the lake. To see them well, you'll need to clamber up through the rocks for a few minutes, taking care not to cut yourself on the sharp edges. There is a great view of the lake from here and you can get a clear shot of the much-photographed rock carvings.

Just beyond Las Caritas, a left turn leads down to the jetty for boats to **Isla Cabritos** (▶ 134). There is a national park ranger station here where you can arrange boats over to the island to observe the crocodiles and flamingoes (see Before You Go). The temperatures here can get very hot, but in a shady grove near the ranger station is a *balneario* or natural swimming pool of cool turquoise mineral water that is ideal for a refreshing dip. Lumbering around are huge iguanas that are quite used to visitors, who they often approach in the hope of getting a snack. Down by the rickety jetty, the bleached branches of trees buried in sand on the shore of the lake create an eerie atmosphere. From here it is just 5km (3 miles) to the next town of **La Descubierta**.

Taking a Break

Enjoy a typical Dominican lunch of *chivo guisado* (goat stew) for around US$1 at one of the food stalls beside the *balneario* at **La Descubierta**.

5–6

La Descubierta has a beautiful stand of towering oak trees sheltering another mineral bathing pool called **Balneario Las Barías**. This one is particularly popular among Dominicans for the beneficial properties of its sulphur waters, and on weekends there is a real holiday atmosphere about the place. People bring picnics; food and drink vendors do good business; and the rhythms of *merengue* and *bachata* fill the air. Continue on Highway 48 around the west shore of the lake to **Jimaní**, just 3km (2 miles) from the Haitian border.

6–7

Jimaní is one of the main border crossing points between the DR and Haiti, open to foreigners too, and it can be interesting to hang around awhile and watch the constant activity – much of it furtive – hinting of a thriving trade in smuggling. Between the two borders is a no man's land where stalls sell second-hand shoes, cooking oil and household implements. On a hill beyond the town, there is a vertical carved ditch on a hill delineating the actual frontier. The town itself is a drab-looking place, and there is little to keep you from completing the Lago Enriquillo Loop along the south side of the lake on Highway 46.

There are few views of the lake from this side, and all around seems barren wilderness, apart from Laguna Limón, a large freshwater lake on the right about 20km (12 miles) from Jimaní. Just beyond this lake, a right branch leads through the village of La Florida and up into the Parque Nacional Sierra de Bahoruco (▶ 134). To return to Barahona, however, keep going east on Highway 46, passing the Enriquillo statue again as you retrace your route to town.

Large, friendly iguanas will approach visitors in the hope of a handout

4 CORDILLERA CENTRAL

Drive

DISTANCE 48km (30 miles)
TIME 2–3 hours
START POINT Jarabacoa ⊞ 181 E3
END POINT Constanza ⊞ 181 D2

For a taste of the lush scenery of the Cordillera Central and a glimpse of the lives of Dominican highlanders, follow this short but tough drive from Jarabacoa to Constanza. You will need a 4WD vehicle, particularly if you attempt it during the rainy season (May–September), when the dirt road can turn to sludge. The route climbs from 500m (1,640 feet) in Jarabacoa to 1,300m (4,264 feet) at Constanza, passing near gushing waterfalls, running along ridges with fantastic views and through tiny villages. For the last 21km (13 miles) into Constanza, it follows a well-surfaced road.

1–2

Begin the drive at **Parque Central** in Jarabacoa. Head east out of town along Calle del Carmen (**Highway 28**), which runs along

the south side of the square. About 3km (2 miles) from the town centre, a signposted turn to the right leads along a bumpy dirt road for another 3km to **Salto de Baiguate** (▶ 147), a small but attractive

waterfall. To visit the waterfall, park up in the car park and walk for 10 minutes along a delightful path hemmed in by dense vegetation. There is often a group of young Dominicans splashing about in the shallow pool at its base.

2–3

Highway 28 is sealed for the first few kilometres from Jarabacoa, but quickly deteriorates into a bumpy dirt track that heads over the hills southward towards Constanza. At 7km (4.5 miles) from

□ **LA VEGA**

Bayacanes ○

Parque Nacional Arqueologico Historico La Vega Vieja

28

○ Buena Vista

■ Salto de Jimenoa

Jarabacoa ○

① ② ■ Salto de Baiguate

■ Salto de Jimenoa Uno ③

28

1556m ▲

Reserva Cientifica Ebano Verde

0 — 5 miles
0 — 10 km

Jarabacoa, the road passes through a small, unnamed village. Just beyond the village, to your right, is a string of shacks, one of which is a *comedor* (simple restaurant). If you'd like to look at the region's most spectacular waterfall, **Salto de Jimena Uno** (▶ 147), park and walk down a track opposite these shacks. The track quickly turns into a steep and narrow footpath that leads across some huge rocks to the base of the falls. The falls themselves are very powerful, sending rainbow-coloured spray shooting up from the deep pond, and if the place looks familiar, you may have seen it in the movie *Jurassic Park*. Take care not to slip as you clamber back up to the vehicle, particularly after rain.

colourful houses and rural people going about their daily tasks. The poor state of the road requires a slow speed, but the views are so attractive that there is no need to hurry and your caution will be appreciated by the occasional horseback riders. Along several stretches, the road follows a ridge that offers superb views of the surrounding countryside, including pine

3–4

Beyond the turning to the waterfall, the rough road climbs steadily, passing small clusters of

One of the many breathtaking views on the road to La Ermita

Taking a Break

There are several small restaurants in Constanza, of which Lorenzo's (➤ 154) offers a good range of Dominican and international dishes.

trees that would be more familiar in a northern climate. Eventually, the road climbs up to a small chapel, La Ermita, built on top of a hill, where candles are on sale for those who wish to pray for a safe journey.

4–5

Beyond La Ermita, the road continues to wind its way southward until it reaches a junction

with Highway 12 at the village of El Río. Turn right here onto a sealed road that runs from Highway 1 just north of Bonao to Constanza. From here the going is much easier, though occasional potholes can still create a hazard. Continue along this road for another 21km (13 miles), and as you arrive in the valley where the town of Constanza is nestled, you will pass fertile fields where all kinds of vegetables and flowers are grown. Check in to a small hotel such as Cabañas de la Montaña for the night. You should still have time for a stroll around the small town and its picturesque surroundings.

Climbing Pico Duarte

If you're looking for a real challenge in the highlands, you could become one of the 3,000 or so people who climb to the top of the highest point in the Caribbean each year – Pico Duarte, 3087m (10,125 feet). The trek takes a minimum of three days and you need to go with an organised tour operated by companies like Maxima Aventura and Iguana Mama (➤ 34). There are several routes to the top of the mountain, but the most popular begins from La Ciénaga, a small village west of Jarabacoa on the Río Yaque del Norte.

When To Go

The trails up the mountain are open all year, but the clearest weather is from December to March.

What To Take

● A sturdy pair of hiking/walking boots, warm clothes (it gets very cold at night!), waterproofs, a walking stick, a flashlight and a medical kit. Your guide will arrange food and water.

● Seriously consider hiring a mule as well as a guide – not only will it free you up to enjoy the walk, but you can also cheat if your legs just won't take it any more.

Horse riders cross the Río Yaque del Norte

Practicalities

GETTING ADVANCE INFORMATION

Websites

- www.webdominicana.com
- www.dr1.com
- www.dominican republic.com
- www.hispaniola.com
- www.dominican-rep.com
- www.lonelyplanet.com

In the UK
Dominican Republic Tourist Board
20 Hand Court
High Holborn London WC1
☎ (020) 7242 7778

BEFORE YOU GO

WHAT YOU NEED

	UK	Germany	USA	Canada	Australia	Ireland	Netherlands	Spain
● Required ○ Suggested ▲ Not required △ Not applicable								
Passport/National Identity Card	●	●	●	●	●	●	●	●
Tourist Card (US$10 payable on arrival)	●	●	●	●	●	●	●	●
Onward or Return Ticket	●	●	●	●	●	●	●	●
Health Inoculations	○	○	○	○	○	○	○	○
Health Documentation	▲	▲	▲	▲	▲	▲	▲	▲
Travel Insurance	○	○	○	○	○	○	○	○
Driving Licence (national)	●	●	●	●	●	●	●	●
Car Insurance Certificate	○	○	○	○	○	○	○	○
Car Registration Document	△	△	△	△	△	△	△	△

WHEN TO GO

Temperatures based on Santo Domingo

High season   Low season

JAN	FEB	MAR	APR	MAY	JUN	JUL	AUG	SEP	OCT	NOV	DEC
25°C	25°C	25°C	25°C	25°C	28°C	28°C	28°C	28°C	28°C	25°C	26°C
77°F	77°F	77°F	77°F	77°F	84°F	84°F	84°F	84°F	84°F	77°F	78°F

☀ Sun   ☁ Cloud   🌧 Wet   ⛅ Sun/Showers

The Dominican Republic is blessed with a climate that makes it an appealing destination at any time of year, though the majority of foreign visitors arrive between **December and April** to avoid the winters in Europe, Canada and the USA. The wet season runs from **May to October**, but this is reversed on the **north coast**, where rain is more likely between **October and May**. Rain is rarely constant and is usually limited to a brief downpour before the skies clear again. From May to October hotel prices are lower and there are fewer visitors. The **high altitudes** of the **Cordillera Central** bring low temperatures at night from **November to February**, though the skies are usually clear in the day. Rain can be more persistent here than in other regions from **May to October**. **Hurricanes** are rare and not usually destructive, but can occur at any time between July and October.

GETTING THERE

From Europe The great majority of visitors to the Dominican Republic (around 80 per cent) are on **all-inclusive holidays** and arrive on charter flights at the nearest airport to their destination. Some charter companies will accept flight-only bookings, depending on last-minute availability, so if you are travelling independently, **it is worth checking out websites** such as www.trailfinders.com and www.opodo.com. There are scheduled direct flights from most European capitals, though none from the UK at the time of writing. Major airlines which fly to the Dominican Republic regularly include Iberia, Air Europa, Air France and Martinair. The flight time is around 8–10 hours.

From North America As with Europe, most visitors from the USA and Canada arrive in the Dominican Republic on charter flights at one of the airports near the all-inclusive resorts at Punta Cana, Playa Dorada and Bayahibe. The majority of scheduled flights from the US leave from **Miami**, though there are several from **New York** as well. In Canada, there are direct flights from **Toronto** and **Montreal**. For information about current offers, check out www.applevacations.com in the USA or www.wholesaletravel.com in Canada. American Airlines is the main carrier in the US, though Continental, Northwest and US Air also fly to the Dominican Republic. Air Canada is the main carrier from Canada. Flight times vary depending on city of departure: from New York it is 4 hours.

From Australia There are no direct flights from Australia to the Dominican Republic, so the most convenient route to take is via New York or Miami (if transiting via the USA) or via London (if transiting via the UK)

TIME

The Dominican Republic is in the Eastern Standard Time Zone of the USA (same as New York), but does not adjust for daylight saving time, so it is five hours behind London in summer (GMT-5) and four hours in winter.

CURRENCY AND FOREIGN EXCHANGE

Currency The basic unit of currency in the DR is the peso (RD$). **Notes** come in denominations of 2,000, 1,000, 500, 100, 50, 20, 10 and 5 pesos. There is also a 1–peso coin. The peso is divided into 100 centavos, and there are **coins** of 50, 25, 10 and 5 centavos, though they are not common. US dollars are widely accepted and many hotels quote their rates in dollars and accept payment in dollars only. In this book hotel and restaurant prices are quoted in US dollars.

Credit Cards are widely accepted throughout the Dominican Republic, and cash machines are common in the tourist centres.

Exchange Cash and travellers' cheques can be exchanged at banks and *casas de cambio* (exchange offices), though it can be difficult to change anything other than US dollars. At the time of going to press, the exchange rate for pesos was extremely volatile, so check out the latest rate at www.xe.com.

TIME DIFFERENCES

GMT	DR	USA New York	Germany	Spain	Australia
12 noon	7am	7am	1pm	1pm	Sydney 10 pm

WHEN YOU ARE THERE

CLOTHING SIZES

UK	Europe	USA/DR	
36	46	36	
38	48	38	
40	50	40	Suits
42	52	42	
44	54	44	
46	56	46	
7	41	8	
7.5	42	8.5	
8.5	43	9.5	Shoes
9.5	44	10.5	
10.5	45	11.5	
11	46	12	
14.5	37	14.5	
15	38	15	
15.5	39/40	15.5	Shirts
16	41	16	
16.5	42	16.5	
17	43	17	
8	34	6	
10	36	8	
12	38	10	Dresses
14	40	12	
16	42	14	
18	44	16	
4.5	38	6	
5	38	6.5	
5.5	39	7	Shoes
6	39	7.5	
6.5	40	8	
7	41	8.5	

NATIONAL HOLIDAYS

1 Jan	New Year's Day
21 Jan	Day of Our Lady of Altagracia
26 Jan*	Duarte Day
27 Feb	Independence Day
Mar/Apr†	Good Friday and Easter Monday
1 May*	Labour Day
May/Jun†	Corpus Christi
16 Aug*	Restoration Day
24 Sep	Day of Our Lady of Las Mercedes
6 Nov*	Constitution Day
25 Dec	Christmas Day

* = celebrated on the nearest Monday to this date.
† = dates vary

OPENING HOURS

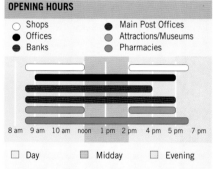

○ Shops
● Offices
● Banks
● Main Post Offices
● Attractions/Museums
● Pharmacies

8 am   9 am   10 am   noon   1 pm   2 pm   4 pm   5 pm   7 pm

□ Day   ■ Midday   □ Evening

Shops Many souvenir and gift shops in tourist areas stay open until 10 or 11 pm, and also open at the weekends. Tourist shops are also more likely to stay open at lunch.
Churches Services are generally held on Sunday morning and evening, but apart from these times, many churches remain locked.
Museums Opening and closing times vary from place to place. Bear in mind that many museums refuse entry to visitors arriving within half an hour of closing time.

EMERGENCY 911

POLICE 911

FIRE 911

AMBULANCE 911

PERSONAL SAFETY

• The DR is generally safe for visitors, but spiralling inflation has occasionally caused national strikes and violent confrontations between protestors and police, so keep an eye on the latest news at: www.news.bbc.co.uk/2/hi/americas

• Women may be subject to the attentions of ultra-macho males. Ignoring them is usually the best policy.

• In the case of criminal acts against tourists, there is a special tourist police force called *Politur*, which can be contacted at 221 4660 (Santo Domingo) and 586 3676 (Puerto Plata).

Police assistance:
📞 **911** from any phone

ELECTRICITY

The power supply in the DR is 110 volts/60 cycles (the same as the USA), so European visitors

tors will need an adaptor. Power cuts are frequent

throughout the country, but the big hotels and resorts have their own generators.

TELEPHONES

There are several private telephone companies in the DR, of which **Codetel** is the most efficient. They have an office in most towns, usually open from 8 am–10 pm, and rates for international calls are very reasonable. Pay after your call with cash or credit card. Many offices also offer internet and fax services. Hotel rates are double or treble those charged by Codetel.

Phone calls within the Dominican Republic
The code for everywhere in the Dominican Republic is 809.

International Dialling Codes
Dial 00 followed by
UK: 44
USA/Canada: 1
Germany: 49
Spain: 34
Australia: 61

POST

The postal system is **incredibly slow and unreliable** – allow at least three weeks for a postcard to reach North America and over a month to reach Europe. All towns have a *correos*, or post office, and in the bigger towns there is an *entrega especial* (special delivery service).

TIPS/GRATUITIES

Hotel and restaurant charges include a 10 per cent service charge, but whether it ever reaches the staff is another matter; so if you are happy with the service, it is a good idea to leave a small tip.

Restaurants	10%
Bar service	Leave change
Taxis	Leave change
Porters	US$1
Chambermaids	US$1 per day
Tour guides	US$2–5

UK
☎ 472 7111

USA
☎ 221 2171

Canada
☎ 685 1136

Germany
☎ 565 8811

Spain
☎ 565 6500

HEALTH

Insurance It is a good idea to take out a travel insurance policy if you are not already covered, but check conditions carefully if you plan to participate in adventure sports like SCUBA diving or white-water rafting, as many policies specifically exclude treatment of injuries from such a cause.

Dental services In the event that you need emergency dental treatment while in the DR, ask your hotel receptionist to direct you to the nearest reliable dental clinic.

Sun Advice The Caribbean sun can be extremely strong, so if you are wise you will avoid exposure to it between 10am and 3pm. You can still get a good suntan in the morning and evening hours, but use a high-factor sunscreen liberally, and also wear a hat and sunglasses when moving about.

Drugs Pharmacies in the DR are easy to find and are generally well-stocked, but if you are taking medication at the time of your visit, it is best to pack sufficient supplies just in case you cannot find it there.

Safe Water Tap water in the DR is **not safe** to drink, so make sure you have a constant supply of bottled water, which is available everywhere at cheap prices. Ice in the big hotels and resorts is quite safe to consume, but it is advisable to avoid it in less expensive local restaurants and cafés.

CONCESSIONS

Students/young people Students travelling with an International Student Identity Card are entitled to discounts in places like museums, however entrance fees are generally very low.

Senior citizens There are no special concessions for senior citizens, yet there are plenty who come back year after year, particularly to the all-inclusive resorts.

TRAVELLING WITH A DISABILITY

Many resorts and hotels have wheelchair access to some rooms and most amenities; check these details carefully before making a reservation. Unfortunately, there are not many facilities for travellers with disabilities elsewhere in the Dominican Republic, though a few of the major monuments have access ramps.

CHILDREN

Dominicans adore children, and if you are travelling with them, it will bring you many chance encounters with the locals. All-inclusive resorts have childcare facilities and loads of activities for kids, which makes this type of holiday so popular with families.

TOILETS

Public toilets are very rare in the DR, and where they exist they are not usually kept clean. Where possible, use facilities in better restaurants or bars. Discard toilet paper in any receptacle provided or you may clog up the plumbing.

CUSTOMS

The import of wildlife souvenirs sourced from rare or endangered species may be either illegal or require a special permit. Before buying, check your home country's customs regulations.

GREETINGS AND COMMON WORDS

Yes/No **Sí/no**
Please **Por favor**
Thank you **Gracias**
You're welcome **De nada**
Hello **Hola**
Goodbye **Adiós**
Good morning **Buenos días**
Good afternoon **Buenas tardes**
Good night **Buenas noches**
How are you? **¿Qué tal?**
Fine, thank you **Bien, gracias**
How much is this? **¿Cuánto vale?**
I'm sorry **Lo siento**
Excuse me **Perdone**
I'd like **Me gustaría**
Open **Abieto**
Closed **Cerrado**
My name is... **Me llamo...**
What's your name? **¿Cómo se llama?**
Pleased to meet you **Mucho gusto**
My pleasure **El gusto es mío**
I'm from... **Soy de...**
Great Britain **Gran Bretaña**
England **Inglaterra**
Scotland **Escocia**
Canada **Canadá**
The United States **Los Estados Unidos**

ACCOMMODATION

Do you have a single/double room?
¿Le queda alguna habitación individual/doble?
with/without bath/toilet/shower
con/sin baño propio/lavabo propio/ducha propia
Does that include breakfast?
¿Incluye desayuno?
Could I see a room? **¿Puedo ver la habitación?**
I'll take this room **Me quedo con esta habitación**
The key to the room..., please **La llave de la habitación..., por favor**
Thank you for your hospitality
Muchas gracias por la hospitalidad

DAYS

Today **Hoy**
Tomorrow **Mañana**
Yesterday **Ayer**
Monday **Lunes**
Tuesday **Martes**
Wednesday **Miércoles**
Thursday **Jueves**
Friday **Viernes**
Saturday **Sábado**
Sunday **Domingo**

DIRECTIONS AND TRAVELLING

I'm lost **Me he perdido**
Where is...? **¿Dónde está?**

How do I get to...? **¿Cómo se va...?**
the bank **al banco**
the post office **a la oficina de correos**
the train station **a la estación de trenes**

Where are the toilets? **¿Dónde están los servicios?**
Left **a la izquierda**
Right **a la derecha**
Straight on **todo recto**
At the corner **en la esquina**

At the traffic-light **en el semáforo**
At the crossroads **en la intersección**
Airport **Aeropuerto**
Boat **Barco**
Bus **Autobus**
Bus station **Estación/terminal**
Car **Automóvil**
Church **Iglesia**
Embassy **Embajada**
Hospital **Hospital**
Market **Mercado**
Museum **Museo**
Street **Calle**
Taxi stand **Parada de taxi**
Ticket **Boleto**

NUMBERS

0 **cero**	10 **diez**	20 **veinte**	200 **doscientos**
1 **uno**	11 **once**	21 **veintiuno**	300 **trescientos**
2 **dos**	12 **doce**	30 **treinta**	400 **cuatrocientos**
3 **tres**	13 **trece**	40 **cuarenta**	
4 **cuarto**	14 **catorce**	50 **cincuenta**	500 **quinientos**
5 **cinco**	15 **quince**	60 **sesenta**	600 **seiscientos**
6 **seis**	16 **dieciséis**	70 **setenta**	700 **setecientos**
7 **siete**	17 **diecisiete**	80 **ochenta**	800 **ochocientos**
8 **ocho**	18 **dieciocho**	90 **noventa**	900 **novecientos**
9 **nueve**	19 **diecinueve**	100 **cien**	1000 **mil**

Useful words and phrases 177

RESTAURANT

I'd like to book a table **¿Me gustaría reservar una mesa?**

A table for **Una mesa para**

Have you got a table for two, please? **¿Tienen una mesa para dos personas, por favor?**

Could we see the menu, please? **¿Nos podría traer la carta, por favor?**

Could I have the bill, please? **¿La cuenta, por favor?**

service charge included **servicio**

incluido

breakfast **el desayuno**

lunch **el almuerzo**

dinner **la cena**

table **una mesa**

waiter/waitress **camarero/camarera**

starters **los entremeses**

main course **el plato principal**

dessert **postres**

dish of the day **plato del dia**

bill **la cuenta**

MENU READER

al carbon barbecued

al horno baked

al mojo de ajo in butter and garlic

al vapor steamed

aceituna olive

agua water

aguacate avocado

ajo garlic

arroz rice

asado roasted

atún tuna

azúcar sugar

bandera dominicana red beans and rice, usually served with chicken, plantain or pork stew

batida fruit shake

bebida drink

bien hecha well-done

bistec steak

bocadillo sandwich

boniato sweet potato

café coffee

caldo soup

camarones shrimp

cangrejo crab

carne meat

cebolla onion

cerdo pork

cerveza beer

champiñones mushroom

chivo guisado goat stew

chorizo spicy

sausage

chuleta chop

cocido stew

cocina kitchen

coco coconut

condimentado (-a) spicy

cordero lamb

cortado (-a) en cubos diced

crudo rare

dulce sweet

ejotes green (French) beans

empanado (-a) breaded

en escabeche marinated

ensalada salad

entremés hors d'oeurve

especialidades de la casa house specialities

especialidades locales local specialities

fideos noodles

filete fillet steak

fricasé meat stew

frijoles beans

fritas fries or chips

frito fried

fruta fruit

gaseosas sodas, carbonated drinks

guayaba guava

hamburguesa hamburger

helado ice cream

hervido boiled

hielo ice

huevo egg

huevos fritos/revueltos fried/scrambled eggs

jamón ham

jugo de fruta fruit juice

langosta lobster

leche milk

lechuga lettuce

legumbres vegetables

limón lemon

maíz corn

malanga taro

mantequilla butter

manzana apple

mariscos seafood

mermelada jam

mofongo plantain, pork rind and garlic dish

mondongo tripe and entrails stew

mortadela sausage

naranja orange

pan bread

papas potato

pepino cucumber

pescado fish

picadillo beef hash

pimienta pepper

piña pineapple

plátano banana

pollo chicken

puerco pork

puré mashed potatoes

queso cheese

res beef

ron rum

rosbif roast beef

sal salt

salchicha sausage

salsa sauce

sopa soup

tasajo salt-dried beef

té tea

ternera veal

tocino bacon

tomate tomato

tortilla omelette

tostada toasted

tostones banana chips

vegetariano vegetarian

vino wine

zanahoria carrot

IF YOU NEED HELP

Help! **¡Socorro!/ ¡Ayuda!**

Could you help me, please? **¿Podría ayudarme, por favor?**

Do you speak English? **¿Habla ingles?**

I don't understand **No comprendo**

I don't speak Spanish **No hablo español**

Could you call a doctor? **¿Podría llamar a un medico, por favor?**

Atlas

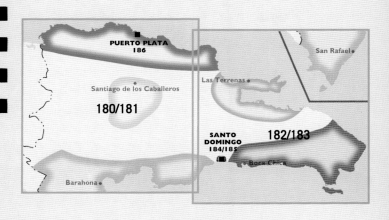

PUERTO PLATA
186

Santiago de los Caballeros

180/181

San Rafael

Las Terrenas

SANTO
DOMINGO
184/185

182/183

Boca Chica

Barahona

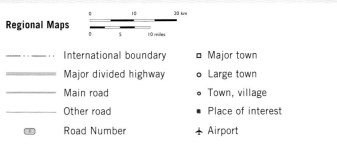

Regional Maps

0 10 20 km	
0 5 10 miles	

— ·· — ·· — International boundary   ▫ Major town

═══════ Major divided highway   ◦ Large town

─────── Main road   ◦ Town, village

─────── Other road   ▪ Place of interest

⬭ Road Number   ✈ Airport

City Plan   **Santo Domingo**

0   200   400   600   800   1000 metres
0   200   400   600   800   1000 yards

Puerto Plata

0   200   400   1000 metres
0   200   400   1000 yards

─────── Main road   ▪ Important building

─────── Other road   ▪ Park

                                       ▪ Featured place of interest

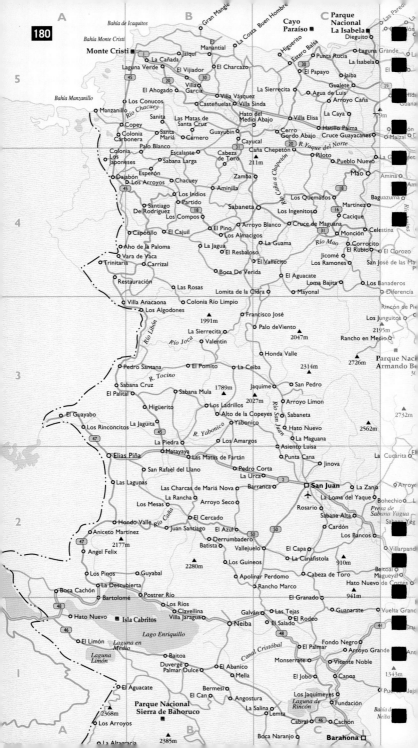

Santo Domingo

Puerto Plata

Picture Credits

The Automobile Association wishes to thank the following photographers, libraries and museums for their assistance with the preparation of this book.

Front and back cover: (t) AA World Travel Library/C. Sawyer; (ct) AA World Travel Library/L. K. Stow; (cb) AA World Travel Library/C. Sawyer; (b) AA World Travel Library/L. K. Stow

CPA/RON EMMONS 27t, 52, 70, 87t, 108, 111t, 128/9, 131, 165, 175l; DOMINIAN REPUBLIC TOURIST BOARD 2(v), 3(iv), 6, 13b, 14c, 15t, 15c, 22c, 23t, 23b, 26c, 55, 58, 83, 85t, 86, 95, 113, 115, 130, 157, 158r, 162; MARY EVANS PICTURE LIBRARY 17t; GETTY IMAGES/HULTON ARCHIVES 10c; GETTY IMAGES/NEWS AND SPORT 28/9.

All remaining images are held in the Association's own library (AA WORLD TRAVEL LIBRARY) and were taken by CLIVE SAWYER with the exception of the following:
D. LYONS 114; L. K. STOW 8b, 9b, 14b, 24/5, 45t, 48, 54t, 54b, 56, 68, 118b, 143, 146, 150, 166

Acknowledgments

Ron Emmons would like to thank Sabrina Cambiaso, Carlos Rafael Batista Velázquez and Prudencio Ferdinand of the Dominican Republic Tourist Board for their generous assistance in researching this book.

SPIRAL GUIDES

Questionnaire

Dear Traveler

Your comments, opinions and recommendations are very important to us. So please help us to improve our travel guides by taking a few minutes to complete this simple questionnaire.

Send to: Spiral Guides, MailStop 66, 1000 AAA Drive, Heathrow, FL 32746–5063

Your recommendations...

We always encourage readers' recommendations for restaurants, nightlife or shopping – if your recommendation is added to the next edition of the guide, we will send you a FREE AAA Spiral Guide of your choice. Please state below the establishment name, location and your reasons for recommending it.

_____

_____

_____

_____

_____

Please send me AAA Spiral_____

(see list of titles inside the back cover)

About this guide...

Which title did you buy?

_____ **AAA Spiral**

Where did you buy it? _____

When? m m / y y

Why did you choose a AAA Spiral Guide? _____

_____

_____

_____

Did this guide meet your expectations?

Exceeded ☐   Met all ☐   Met most ☐   Fell below ☐

Please give your reasons _____

_____

_____

_____

continued on next page...

Were there any aspects of this guide that you particularly liked?

Is there anything we could have done better?

About you...

Name (Mr/Mrs/Ms)

Address

Zip

Daytime tel nos.

Which age group are you in?

Under 25 ☐   25–34 ☐   35–44 ☐   45–54 ☐   55–64 ☐   65+ ☐

How many trips do you make a year?

Less than one ☐   One ☐   Two ☐   Three or more ☐

Are you a AAA member? Yes ☐   No ☐

Name of AAA club

About your trip...

When did you book? m m / y y   When did you travel? m m / y y

How long did you stay?

Was it for business or leisure?

Did you buy any other travel guides for your trip? ☐ Yes   ☐ No

If yes, which ones?

Thank you for taking the time to complete this questionnaire.